Mastering

Your Nexus 7

Nexus-7 HD 2013 LTE Model
Android 4.4.2 (KitKat)

George Root

Mastering Your Nexus 7

by George Root

Copyright © 2014 George Root. All rights reserved

March 2014: First Edition

ISBN-13: 978-1496070869
ISBN-10: 1496070860

Table of Contents

Preface

About the Author

Hi, my name is **George Root**.

I graduated with an MSEE degree from Caltech back in the dark ages before there were personal computers. I began my career in the aerospace industry starting with the big mainframe computers from Univac, IBM, and DEC. During my career I have written thousands of pages of technical documentation. But writing this book on the Google Nexus-7 has been one of my most enjoyable writing project.

In 1985 I saw a demonstration of a new type of computer called a "Macintosh". It immediately struck me that this was the way computers were supposed to work. I bought a Mac and ever since then I have been a fan of, some might say fanatic about, Apple computers.

Then one day, not long ago, a friend asked me what I knew about Chrome computers. I knew that there was a web browser from Google called Chrome, but I didn't know there was also a Chrome Operating System (OS) and that computers were being built to run that OS. I started reading about Chrome and was once again struck by the thought "this is the way computers are supposed to work".

Android is the tablet / phone version of Chrome and it brings many of the advantages of the Chrome OS to portable devices. Your Nexus-7 is run by the Android OS.

I hope you find this book useful and join me in my admiration for the work that Google has put into Android and the Nexus devices. If you do find this book useful, I would appreciate it if you would stop by the Amazon Book Store and give it a good review. Thanks!

I am not affiliated in any way with Google except as a customer.

You can send me feedback about this book at:

NexusBookFeedback@gmail.com

Why Did I Write this Book?

To tell the truth I didn't set out to write a book about Nexus tablets. I really wanted to buy one. I recently bought a Google Nexus-7 tablet and began trying to figure out how to use it. I wanted a book to tell me how to set up and use all of the nifty new features of Android. Google's approach to computing is different in several ways from using an "ordinary" personal computer and I needed a guide to help me through the learning process. Perhaps you feel the same way.

Unable to find a book that answered all of my questions, I ended up researching hundreds of Google Nexus Support web pages. At the same time I was experimenting with my Nexus-7 and trying to put into practice what I was learning. Some of these experiments were less than successful. It occurred to me that I might not be the only one who needed a little help getting to know the Nexus-7 and that an up-to-date Nexus book might be useful to other people like me.

Google Chrome and Android are moving targets - they are constantly evolving and improving. New features are added. Old features are updated. The contents of this book are up to date as of March 2014, the Nexus-7 (2013 LTE model) and Android version 4.4.2 (KitKat), but some things may be different by the time you read this. Hopefully those differences will be small.

What You Will Find in this Book

In this book I will discuss setting up and using the Nexus-7 2013 LTE model.

I know that you are anxious to learn all about your new Nexus-7, but there are some things that you should know in order better to understand how the Nexus-7 fits into the big Google Cloud Computing universe. The Nexus-7 is just a portal into that universe, and it will make things clearer and more useful to understand a little about how Google cloud computing works. So the first chapter will introduce the Google Cloud Computing universe. And then we will look through the Nexus portal into that universe in the following chapters.

Although this is a book about the Nexus-7 Android tablet, there are a couple of things you will need to do on your personal computer to prepare for using the Nexus. To get the maximum utility out of your Nexus-7, you will need to have a Google Account. You cannot access the Google Cloud Computing universe without an account. Setting up a Google Account is much easier on your personal computer than it is on the Nexus-7 itself. There are also some aspects of account security that you cannot set up on the Nexus-7 itself. So, Chapter 2 will lead you through the process of setting up a new Google Account using your personal computer.

If you want to print from your Nexus-7 tablet, you will have to set up your printer using your personal computer. There are three different ways to print from your Nexus-7 and Chapter 3 will explain each of them and what you have to do to set up your chosen printing method.

The remainder of this book, beginning with Chapter 4, will explain setting up and working with your Nexus-7 and I have tried to organize this material more or less in the same order you would need the information if you were starting out with a new Nexus-7.

The Google "universe" is huge and no single book can cover all of the services Google provides. I will concentrate on those for which there are apps in the standard Android installation.

NOTE: Essentially all of the figures shown in this book have been edited to reduce the amount of space needed to display them. So, in many cases what you see on your Nexus-7 screen will not look exactly like the figures used in this book. In some cases I have added labels that do not appear on the Nexus screen in order to make things a little clearer. I hope you don't find these changes confusing.

1 - Google Cloud Computing

1.1 - What the Heck is "Google Cloud Computing"?

To many people "Google" is the search engine that we all use to find stuff on the web. But in the background, Google, the company, has been inventing "The Next Big Thing" in computer technology and it is revolutionizing the way computing will be done in the future.

All of the classical personal computers that we are familiar with, Macs and PCs, were invented before there was an internet. In those days, each computer was an island unto itself. Because of this, all of the apps and all of the data associated with those apps were stored on the computer itself. This required large amounts of internal storage and fast - read "expensive" - computers.

Google invented itself after the internet was commonly available to people who owned personal computers and Google saw a different way to do things making use of the internet. Google saw that the internet made it possible to have powerful apps and huge amounts of data that resided, not on people's personal computers, but rather on servers connected to the internet. Now days, we refer to these computers on the internet as being in the "cloud". The implication of the word "cloud" is that the computers are out there somewhere, but we really don't have to know where just so long as we can communicate with them over the internet.

This idea, that apps and their associated data could reside on servers in the cloud, made possible a completely different concept of personal computers. With cloud computing, the personal computer could be very simple - basically just a web browser like Safari, Internet Explorer, or Google Chrome. The computer would send requests to the cloud computers and those cloud computers would do all of the heavy lifting needed to perform the necessary computations and then they would send the results of those computations back to the requesting personal computer. With this approach, the personal computer could be very simple - read "inexpensive". It wouldn't need much internal storage nor would it require powerful processors. All of the apps and data could reside in the cloud. All the personal computer would need to do is be able to send requests and display the results sent back by the "cloud".

You are probably already using cloud computing perhaps without realizing it. Whenever you shop on Amazon, it is the Amazon servers that are doing all of the hard work. All your computer does is display the results of those computations.

To implement this concept of cloud computing, Google has constructed an enormous system of servers all around the world. They have developed a new operating system (OS) named "Chrome" and a family of simple cloud based computers that run the Chrome OS. These computers are known generically as "Chromebooks" for the laptop versions. The Google Nexus-7 is one of a class of tablet computers that run the mobile version of Chrome which is called "Android".

I should mention that the "Chrome" web browser that you may have installed on your personal computer is not the same as the Chrome OS. The Chrome web browser runs on ordinary personal computers. The Chrome OS runs on special computers that are designed specifically to run the Chrome OS. You can experience many of the features of the Chrome OS using the Chrome browser on your current personal computer, but to realize all of the benefits of Chrome, you need to use a computer running the Chrome OS or a mobile device, such as the Nexus-7, running the Android mobile version of Chrome.

This is an exciting time in the world of Chrome and Android devices. The Samsung Chromebook has been the best selling computer on Amazon for months, and the number of vendors making Chrome and Android devices is expanding daily.

I should mention that all Chrome and Android devices are not created equal. There is a "pure" Chrome computer named the "Pixel" designed by Google and running a "pure" version of Chrome. There are also "pure" Android devices designed by Google and running "pure" versions of Android. These are the Nexus phones and tablets. But there are dozens of other computers and mobile devices running versions of Chrome and Android that have been modified by the hardware vendors to provide enhanced features or to match the capabilities of their hardware. The advantage of this is that these devices can offer more features or better performance than the "pure" Android Nexus devices. The downside is that, when Google develops a new version of Android, Nexus devices get that update directly from Google. But for devices from other vendors, the Android upgrade goes to the vendor of the device which must then modify their version of Android to match their device's capabilities. Sometimes these vendors may take weeks, or months, or forever to release the upgrade. That is why you will find some Android devices still running obsolete versions of Android. It's not that the user failed to upgrade Android, but rather that the vendor of the hardware has failed to.

1.2 - What Are Some Advantages of Google Cloud Computing?

There is a wealth of applications (apps) that run on the Nexus-7. But these apps, for the most part, don't reside on your Nexus-7 itself. The revolutionary aspect of Google Cloud Computing is that most of the app software resides on Google servers somewhere in the "cloud". Your documents aren't stored on your Nexus-7 either, but on the Google cloud servers. There are many advantages to this approach. A few of them are:

1.2.1 - Inexpensive hardware and software

The Nexus-7 has limited onboard memory (16 or 32 GB) and it doesn't need a lot of CPU horsepower since all of the heavy lifting is done on and by Google, or other website, servers. So the local hardware is relatively simple and inexpensive. The Android OS is free. Most of the apps are free. Upgrades to Android and all the apps are free. Storage on Google servers is also free (for the first 15GB).

To quantify just how inexpensive the Nexus-7 really is, the current price for the 16 GB WiFi only model is $229 although they can be found for $200 at some stores. In comparison, the Apple iPad Mini with the same 16 GB and WiFi only is $399 - nearly twice as expensive as the Nexus-7.

1.2.2 - Security

Perhaps the biggest advantage of Google Cloud Computing is security.

The major part of the software resides on Google servers so it is difficult, but not impossible, to infect your Nexus-7. Local apps are heavily sandboxed limiting their ability to interact with other app's data. If Google detects a weakness in Android, it gets patched quickly, and your version of Android gets patched automatically at the same time. You don't have to do anything. That phrase "You don't have to do anything" is perhaps the biggest security advantage of Android. Google takes care of everything.

The fact that very little data are stored on your Nexus-7 is a big security advantage. If your Nexus-7 gets lost or stolen or simply fails, all you lose is the hardware. All of your data - think company secrets - is still safely stored on the Google servers. You can recover those data just by signing-in to your Google Account from any other computer in the world.

Everything that gets transmitted between your Android Device and the Google servers, as well as all your synced data that is stored on the Google servers, is (optionally) encrypted. And backed up. Automatically. Once again, you don't have to do anything.

Google has also taken the next step in password protection. Google calls it "2-Step Verification". The idea is that your Google Account password is just a single verification factor. Your password is something that you know (hopefully). Google adds something that you own - your mobile phone - as a second factor needed in order to sign-in to your Google Account. Two-Step Verification can still work if you don't own a mobile phone or if your mobile phone gets lost or stolen. I will explain the details of how all this works in Section 2.3.2.

1.2.3 - Always in Sync

When you create a Google document - a word processing document, a spreadsheet, a slide presentation, or any of the other document types that Android provides - that document gets stored on Google servers. As you work on your document, Android automatically saves it to the Google servers every few seconds. This means that you can sign-in to your Google Account from any computer and you will see exactly the same stuff that was there when you last signed-out even if that was on a different computer. In fact all of your Google Account information is stored on Google servers so that you can sign-in from any computer and everything you see will look just like it did when you last left it. All of your apps, settings, bookmarks, contacts, email messages, calendar events, and documents will be there. All in sync - all automatically.

In some cases a local copy of a document is retained on your Nexus-7 so that you can work on it even if you don't have Internet access. This document will be sent back to the Google servers as soon as your Internet access is re-established.

1.3 - Concerns About Using Google Cloud Computing

There are two primary concerns about using Google Cloud Computing:

1.3.1 - What Happens If I Don't Have an Internet Connection?

Without an Internet connection the Nexus-7 loses much, but not all of its functionality. Clearly, you cannot listen to Pandora Radio nor stream YouTube videos without the Internet. But Google is working to enable some of its apps to function without an Internet connection. Google "Docs", the word processor, can create, display, and edit word processing Docs while offline. These Docs will be automatically uploaded to the Google servers when a connection is re-established. Google "Sheets", the spreadsheet app, can display and edit sheets offline, but cannot create them while offline (yet). Google Calendar can be viewed while offline.

In addition, Google is introducing "Packaged Apps" in the Google "Play" store that developers can create and which can function without the Internet.

The fact is that most of what typical users do on their current personal computers such as: email, web browsing, shopping, FaceBook, Twitter, YouTube, Skype, etc, all require an Internet connection to function. In this respect the Nexus-7 is no different than any other personal computer.

1.3.2 - What About Data Security? Is My Data Safe on Google Servers?

The short answer is that your data is probably safer on Google servers than it is on your current personal computer. All of your synced data stored on Google servers is (optionally) encrypted. All communication between your Android device and Google is encrypted. Everything on the Google servers gets backed up regularly. Access to your data is protected by 2-Step Verification. In all these respects your data with Google is safer than it would be on your own computer.

The real concern is not that some hacker will somehow gain access to your information, but rather that Google will. There is no doubt that Google uses your information for its own purposes - mainly to sell advertising. However, Google clearly states what information it collects about you and why it does that. Google has recently announced that it will no longer provide user information to law enforcement agencies without a probable cause warrant issued by a court.

Briefly, here is the type of information Google collects:

The information you supply when you sign up for a Google Account or a Google Profile: your name, email address, telephone number, age, and photo. Information about the hardware you are using such as the type of computer you are using, the OS you are using, and your IP address. Search queries you submit to the Google search engine. Crash reports including hardware and browser information. Telephone information including your phone number, and the number you are calling, the date, time, and duration of the call. Google will place cookies on your computer that will identify your browser and Google account. If you are using Google Maps on a mobile device Google will collect information about your location and nearby WiFi access points.

All of this is explained in the Google Privacy Policy which you can read here:

http://www.google.com/policies/privacy/

You must agree to all of this in order to set up a Google Account. If you are not comfortable with all this, don't buy a Nexus or Chrome device because, without a Google Account, these devices lose most of their usefulness.

2 - Setting Up a New Google Account

Although you can run your Nexus-7 without a Google Account, you will be missing most of the advantages of Google Cloud Computing since you will not be able to create nor store anything on Google servers. None of your work will be saved nor backed up. Basically, if you don't want to create a Google Account, you have already made two mistakes: 1) you shouldn't have purchased a Nexus-7 and, 2) you shouldn't have purchased this book.

If you have a Gmail address, you already have a Google Account. But even if you already have a Google Account, you might want to read this chapter since it discusses some topics with which you may not be familiar. Like 2-Step Verification, and Application Specific Passwords.

You can create a new Google Account directly on your Nexus-7, but there are some aspects of account security that you cannot set up on the Nexus-7 itself. So, this chapter will lead you through the process of setting up a new Google Account using your personal computer.

But first:

Before you can complete some of the following steps, you must download and install the free Chrome Browser on your personal computer. Get this "Chrome" at:

<u>https://www.google.com/intl/en/chrome/browser/</u>

2.1 - Choosing a Strong Password

The password you choose for your new Google Account will become the password for your Gmail account as well as for your entire Google world. Anyone with this password will be able to access everything you have entrusted to Google from any computer in the world. That is assuming you don't set up 2-Step Verification. I will describe how to set up 2-Step Verification in section 2.3.2. But even with 2-Step Verification turned on, a strong password is still very important. One of the features Google provides when you set up 2-Step Verification is a "Trust This Computer the Next Time" button. When you click this button, Google will go through the 2-Step Verification process only the first time you use that specific computer. Thereafter, you, and anyone else, will be able to sign into your accounts on that computer using only this password. So choose wisely!

Choosing a strong password is really much simpler than you might think. The "old" recommendations were to use a random combination of upper and lower case letters along with numbers and symbols thereby making passwords impossible to remember and thereby creating a lot of business for password manager apps.

Turns out that all of that advice is baloney. Mathematically, the single factor that determines a password's "strength" is the number of characters in it. "Strength" is a measure of how long it would take to break the password using a brute force attack. A password with 12 all lower case letters is an order of magnitude "stronger" than one with only 8 random characters using upper and lower case letters, number, and symbols.

So, choosing unbreakable passwords is really fairly simple. "ILove!Google" - 12 characters both upper and lower case and a punctuation character (!) - is an excellent password. "IReally!LoveGoogle" - 18 characters - is unbreakable yet easy to remember. Invent your own passphrase.

Hackers get passwords now, not by breaking them, but by stealing them - for example by gaining access to insecure vendor accounts and stealing the account passwords. A password manager doesn't protect against this, making their random passwords no more safe than the easily remembered variety.

The most recent password thinking is that passwords are not really that secure even if they are unbreakable, because it is getting easier and easier to just steal them via key loggers or using "social engineering" to convince the user, or a customer service representative, to give the password to the hacker.

Using a strong password is "1-Step Verification" that you are the true owner of this Google account. Google has added a second layer of security by allowing "2-Step Verification" which I will discuss a little later in the setup process (see section 2.3.2).

2.2 - Creating a New Google Account

Start creating a new Google Account by going to the Google account sign up page at:

https://accounts.google.com/SignUp

In the upper right corner of the page that opens, click on the big red "Sign Up" button. This will take you to the actual account creation page. The portion of this webpage where you actually enter your information looks like this:

Entering your real name should be obvious, but choosing your "username" may be more difficult. You cannot have the same username as anyone else who has, or who ever had, a Gmail account. So you may have to get a little creative here. You can use letters, numbers, and "dots" in your user name. Usernames are not case sensitive so "myName" is the same as "myname".

Notice that your Gmail address is composed of the username you choose prepended to the @gmail.com domain name. You can sign-in to Google accounts using only your username. You don't have to include the @gmail.com part, although if you do everything will still work properly.

One of the most important parts of creating your Google account is choosing a strong password. I explained how to do this in Section 2.1 above. Pick a good passphrase and enter it here.

You may choose whether or not to give Google your correct birthday. I would give a false birthday close to your true one. Birthdays are becoming more popular as means to confirm your identity, particularly with health care providers, so I would not hand out this information freely. If you enter a gender, Google will refer to you as he or she. If you choose "Other" instead, Google will use gender neutral terms when referring to you. Google uses this information to send you appropriate advertising.

Giving your correct mobile phone number is essential because Google will use this number to send you the verification codes you will need to sign-on to your account when you have enabled 2-Step Verification. If you don't have a mobile phone you can still use 2-Step Verification by printing out verification codes as I will describe shortly.

Giving your correct "current email address" is also important because Google will send important account messages to the address you give. This cannot be the same Gmail address you are creating with this account.

Below the portion of the Account Creation page I have shown on the previous page, there are a couple more things to enter. You must agree to the Google "Terms of Service" and confirm that you are not a robot trying to create Gmail accounts from which to send spam. If you intend to use Google + (Google's social site - like FaceBook), then you might want to enable the "Google may use my account information to personalize +1 ..." button.

After filling in all of your information, click on the big blue "Next Step" button in the lower right corner of the page. This will take you to a page where you have the opportunity to add a photo to your account. After you do this, should you choose to, click on the blue "Next Step" button which will take you to a "Welcome!" page. From here, clicking on the blue "Get Started" button will take you to your account summary page and you're good to go.

2.3 - Securing Your Google Account

2.3.1 - Turn On Encryption for Your Account

You can select which items: apps, passwords, bookmarks, etc, Google will keep in sync for you. It does this by storing your items on Google servers. You can choose whether these data should be encrypted on the Google servers.

To select which items get synced and whether or not to use encryption, follow these steps:

1) Click on the "Chrome Menu" (the 3-horizontal bar icon at the top right corner of the browser window) and select "Settings"

2) Click on "Advanced Sync Settings" near the top of the page that opens.

3) In the dialog that opens, put a check in the boxes next to the items you want to sync. Or, you can do as I did and just select "Sync Everything"

4) Select whether to encrypt just passwords, or all of your synced data. I chose "Encrypt all synced data". I don't see any reason not to.

5) In the last box choose whether to use your Google Account passphrase as the encryption key. You can also choose to use a different passphrase. If you choose to use a different passphrase, you will have to enter it every time you use a new Chrome browser. You may want to sign-in to your account from a different computer months from now, so you will have to remember this passphrase in addition to your Google Account passphrase.

2.3.2 - How Does "2-Step Verification" Work?

Two-Step Verification is relatively new to Google and some aspects of it may have changed by the time you read this. I strongly recommend that you click on the "Learn More" button in the figure on the next page to be taken on a Google guided tour of 2-Step Verification and how it works. I will summarize the current information here, but for the latest information directly from Google, you should "Learn More".

Basically 2-Step Verification verifies that you are the true owner of the account by requiring that you have two things: 1) the correct password for the account, and 2) the mobile phone whose number you gave to Google when you created your account.

So, this is how you sign in when 2-Step Verification is enabled: When you go to the Sign-In page for any Google service like Gmail, you enter your User Name (with or without the @gmail.com - it makes no difference) and Passphrase. Remember, your user name is not case sensitive, "myname" is the same as "MyName", but the password is case sensitive.

At this point you have a very important decision to make. At the bottom of every "Sign-In" page right next to the "Sign-In" button there is a checkbox labeled "Stay signed in". If you check this box, and **it is checked by default**, anyone who has access to that computer will also have access to everything you have in your Google account. No passwords, no mobile phones needed. So you need to make a choice at this point, do you want your account to be secure, or do you want the convenience of never having to enter your user name and password again. If you are using a public computer such as at a library or at an Internet cafe, always, I repeat **ALWAYS**, make sure this box is not checked before you click the "Sign-In" button. If you are using a laptop, always make sure this box is not checked before you click the "Sign-In" button. If your laptop were lost or stolen anyone who has the laptop will also have access to all of your Google stuff. Personally, I always un-check this box. True I have to sign in every time I go to Google, but I am confident that nobody else can sign-in to my account.

OK. You have un-checked the "Stay Signed In" box and clicked on the "Sign-In" button. If you have entered the correct password, Google will then send an SMS text message to your mobile phone. This message will be a 6-digit number. Meanwhile, back at your computer, there will be a window asking you to enter that 6-digit number. Go ahead and enter the number, but before you click on "Verify" there is another decision to make.

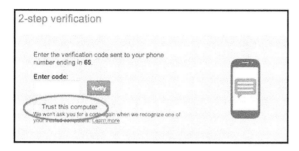

If you do NOT check the "Trust this Computer" box, you will have to go through the whole 2-Step Verification process every time you Sign-In on this computer. If you DO check this box, you will be able to Sign-In using only your user name and password in the future on this computer.

Personally, I do check the "Trust this Computer" box. My account is still protected by my password and if my Nexus were stolen, I could simply change that password using a different computer and that would re-enable the 2-Step Verification process on the stolen Nexus. Whether or not you check "Trust this Computer", nobody else in the world can sign into your Google account from a different computer without access to your mobile phone.

What if you lose your mobile phone, or you don't have mobile phone coverage where you need it? I'll explain how Google solves this problem shortly (see section 2.3.4).

2.3.3 - Set-Up "2-Step Verification"

OK - that's how 2-Step Verification works. Now, how do you set it up? Start setting up 2-Step Verification by going here:

https://www.google.com/settings/security

The account security page that opens has so much stuff on it, that I will not show the entire page, but only those portions I am going to discuss. Be sure to look at those portions that I don't discuss.

The 2-Step Verification part of the Account Security page looks like this:

Because 2-Step Verification is relatively new, and things may have changed after I wrote this, I suggest that you click on the "Learn More" button shown in this figure to get the latest information directly from Google.

At the right side of this figure, there is a button labeled "Settings". Click this button to take you to the 2-Step Verification Settings page. You will have to re-enter your password. And this will bring you to a dialog with a big blue "Start Setup" button. Click this button and you will finally arrive at the page where you will set up 2-Step Verification.

Setting up 2-Step Verification is a four step process:

Step 1: On the first page of this process you will be asked to confirm the mobile phone number you want verification codes sent to. This will be the phone number you entered when you created your account. You also select whether you want the 6-digit access codes sent via SMS text message or by voice call. I chose the SMS message option and it works very well. I find it useful that the 6-digit code stays on the screen of my mobile phone until I have time to enter it on my computer.

Once you have made your choice, click on "Send Code". This will send an access code to your phone and take you to the Step 2 page.

Step 2: On this page you will enter the 6-digit code you received on your phone. Just type it in where it says "Enter Verification Code" and click "Verify". This takes you to the Step 3 page.

Step 3: On the Step 3 page you get to choose whether to "Trust this Computer". "Trusted" computers only ask for an access code the first time you sign in. After that, they only ask for your user name and password. Google recommends that "you make this a trusted computer only if you trust the people who have access to it". Good advice! If you do "trust this computer", click on the checkbox and then click on "Next". This will take you to the Step 4 page.

Step 4: This is the confirmation page. By clicking on "Confirm", you are confirming that you really do want to turn 2-Step Verification ON for this computer and this account.

At this point you have turned on 2-Step Verification, but you're not done yet. When you click on "Confirm" on the Step 4 page, you will be taken to a page with a lot of content. I'm going to refer to this page as the "2-Step Verification is ON" page because that's what you see at the top of the page.

Once again, you will need to return to this page in the future. The easiest way to do this is to return to the account security page:

https://www.google.com/settings/security

and click on "Settings" in the 2-Step Verification portion of the page.

This page has so much content that I will only be able to show it in pieces. Two of those pieces are critical - do not skip the next two sections!

2.3.4 - Generate and Print "Backup Codes"

You now have 2-Step Verification turned on, but suppose you lose your mobile phone or you just don't have mobile coverage when you need it. Google provides a backup plan called "Backup Codes". Here's the pertinent portion of the "2-Step Verification is ON" page.

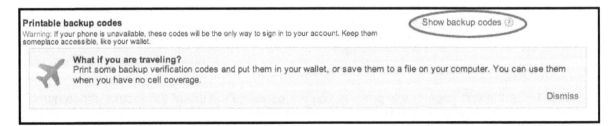

Click on "Show Backup Codes". This will generate a set of 10 Backup Codes, as illustrated in the figure below, which you can print and keep in a safe place. You can use one of these codes in place of one 6-digit verification code sent to your phone. Each code can be used only once. The idea is that you will carry these printed codes with you when you are traveling and might be without mobile phone coverage.

If you use all 10 backup codes or perhaps you lose them, you can generate more at:

https://accounts.google.com/SmsAuthConfig

Don't try to generate and print more than one set of 10 Backup Codes. Each time you generate a new set, the older sets are invalidated.

2.3.5 - How Do You Use "Backup Codes"?

It's quite simple. When you are going through the 2-Step Verification process and you come to the point where you are asked to enter the 6-digit code sent to your mobile phone, but you don't have your mobile phone, just enter one of the backup codes you have printed and carried with you. You have carried them with you haven't you? Each backup code can be used only once so cross off the one you used.

2.3.6 - Setting Up Google Authenticator

With 2-Step Verification enabled, you will need a secret one-time verification code to sign-in to your Google Account in addition to the usual User Name and Password. Normally, this verification code is delivered to you via text message on your mobile phone. But, what if you don't have mobile data service where you are? To handle this situation, Google has provided two different ways to obtain a verification code without mobile phone service. The first method is to generate and print out "Backup Codes" as explained in Section 2.3.4 above.

There is a second way to obtain a verification code without having to carry one around with you. This method still requires that you have a smart phone, but it does not require that you actually have mobile phone coverage at the time. This second method relies on a smart phone app called "Google

Authenticator". There are Google Authenticator apps available for iPhones, Android phones and Blackberries.

So, the first step in using Google Authenticator is to install the appropriate app on your smart phone. You must also have Two-Step Verification enabled for your Google Account, else this whole discussion is pointless.

Initializing Google Authenticator

After you have installed the Google Authenticator app on your smart phone, you have to go to the Google Security page for your Google Account to initialize it. One way to get to this security page is to open any Google service, such as Gmail and sign-in. In the upper-right corner of this window, you will find your Gmail account name where "Click Here", is illustrated in the figure at the left. Click on this

name and a menu will drop down with a few options as shown in this figure. Click on the "Account" item shown outlined in the figure.

Clicking on the "Account" item Illustrated in this figure will take you to to a menu of Account topics. Click on "Security" and this will take you to a page with a lot of Security settings, a portion of which is shown in the figure below. If your 2-Step Verification "Status" is not "ON", go back to Section 2.3.2 and read all about Google 2-Step Verification. You might want to enable it here.

Click on "Edit" as illustrated in the figure at the right and that will take you another page with several options, one of which is named "Mobile Application" as shown in the figure below. Select the type of smart phone you want to set-up with Google Authenticator. In my case, I selected "iPhone".

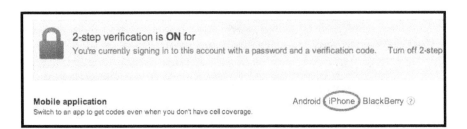

This will finally take you to the page where you can initialize your mobile phone to provide Google Authenticator Backup Codes. This page is illustrated in the top figure on the next page. The first part of this page just tells you that you must have the Google Authenticator app installed on your mobile phone before going any further.

The real action starts with the instructions:

1) In Google Authenticator, tap "+", and then "Scan Barcode"

2) Use your phone's camera to scan this barcode.

Since I have already done these steps, the "+" and "Scan Barcode" buttons don't appear in the figure below-right, but they will when you go through these steps.

So, launch the Google Authenticator app on your mobile phone. Then tap on the "+" to add (generate) another authenticator code and then "Scan Barcode". Now just point your phone's camera at the barcode displayed on your computer screen, just like the one shown in this figure. You may have to move your camera in and out until it focuses properly on the barcode. When the camera is happy with what it sees, it will take the picture automatically - you don't have to do anything.

When the camera takes the picture of the barcode, a number will appear on the screen of your mobile phone. Type this number into the space labeled "Code:" in the figure at the right and then click on "Verify and Save". This will complete the setup process. You will get a confirmation that the setup has finished successfully.

Google Authenticator will now be running on your mobile phone. Whenever you launch the app, it will generate a new Backup Code and display it as illustrated in the figure on the right.

These Backup Codes are valid for 1 minute. After that time, a new Backup Code will be generated. The little clock icons shown circled in the right side of the iPhone screen will count down the 1 minute interval during which the displayed Backup Code remains valid. During the last few seconds remaining, the clock will turn red to let you know that you don't have enough time remaining to enter this Backup Code into whatever app is asking for it, and you should wait until the next code appears.

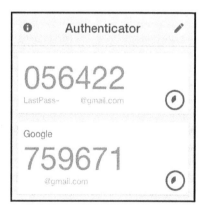

So, the process for using Google Authenticator goes something like this:

- On your personal computer or Nexus-7, you attempt to sign-in to some app that requires Two-Step Verification. That app asks you to enter a 6-digit code that normally would be sent to your mobile phone as a text message. But, since you don't have mobile phone service at this location, that won't work.

- So, you launch the Google Authenticator app on your mobile phone instead. A new 6-digit code will be displayed just as in figure above. Enter this 6-digit number where the original app on your Nexus-7 is asking for it.

Once again, if you take too long to enter the code number given by Authenticator, you will have to wait until a new number is displayed on the Authenticator screen. You will then have 1 minute to enter this number on your Nexus-7.

The Verification Codes generated by Google Authenticator are time based, so this process only works if your mobile phone is set to the correct time.

The figure on the previous page shows another interesting factoid: Google Authenticator works with 3rd-party apps that use Two-Step Verification - not just Google apps. One such 3rd-party app is LastPass, my favorite password manager. Clearly, a password manager needs to have a means of secure sign-in. So, LastPass has adopted the Google Authenticator approach to Two-Step Verification. DropBox is another service that uses Google Authenticator. So, looking back at the figure on the previous page, you can see that this instance of Google Authenticator has generated two verification codes: one for Google (759671), and one for LastPass (056422). Pretty slick!

You set up these 3rd-party apps just as you do for the Google apps that I have described but with the exception that you must go to the 3rd-party app's website to get the proper QR code to scan. For example, the LastPass website is illustrated in this figure.

Once you start using Google Authenticator, you will no longer receive the 6-digit access codes via text or voice message from Google. When one of these access codes is required, just launch Google Authenticator and use the 6-digit code that it creates for you.

2.3.7 - Generate and Print "Application Specific Passwords"

Google's 2-Step Verification is a new feature of Chrome. So new in fact that a few applications that sign-in to your Google account to work, including some from Google itself, are not capable of using it yet. Examples include: mobile Gmail, Apple Mail, Apple iOS Mail, Outlook and Thunderbird. There are also 3rd party apps that access your Google account to run properly. These include 3rd party apps that access Picasa. These apps will ask for your Google password, but your actual password won't work. You have to use an "Application Specific Password" instead of your real Google password. So you must generate and print out a list of Application Specific Passwords.

To get started we, once again, return to the "2-Step Verification is ON" page. The easiest way to do this is to return to the account security page:

https://www.google.com/settings/security

and click on "Settings" in the 2-Step Verification portion of the page.

Here's the pertinent portion of that page:

While on this page, you may wish to click on "Learn More" to learn more about Application Specific Passwords directly from Google. Click on "Manage Application Specific Passwords" to actually generate them. This will take you to this figure:

Google calls these codes "Application Specific Passwords", but the reality is that they are not specific to any particular application. So, there is no need to try and figure out how many applications you have that will require an Application Specific Password. I suggest that you generate and print at least 10 at this time. A particular Application Specific Password can be used for any application that needs one, but it can be used only once.

To generate a single Application Specific Password, type in a name - once again the name isn't important. Any Application Specific Password can be used for any application. So, to save typing, and brain cells, just type simple names. Including numbers will be useful to keep track of how many you have generated and later how many you have used.

Type a name and click "Generate Password". That will take you to a page like this:

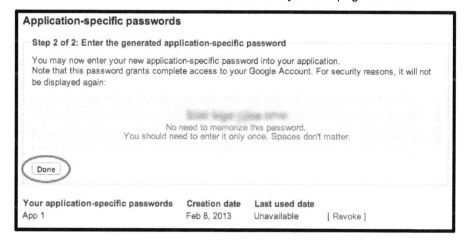

When Google says "No need to memorize this password", they are assuming that you will wait until you are asked for an Application Specific Password and that you will then go through this process of generating one at that time. You would then be able to copy-and-paste the new Application Specific Password into the application asking for it. This is a pretty cumbersome process to go through, especially on your Nexus-7, so I prefer to generate and print several Application Specific Passwords on my personal computer before I actually need them.

If you choose to print a set of Application Specific Passwords, print the page illustrated above so that you will have it when you need it. When you have printed this page, click "Done" and you will be taken back to the previous figure where you can enter a new name and hit "Generate Password" to create the next password. Once again, I suggest you generate at least 10 of these now.

Take care to protect these Application Specific Passwords. They are the only password needed for the app you have used them for. In addition, any of the unused passwords can be used to "unlock" any application that needs an Application Specific Password. They, in effect, bypass the 2-Step Verification process.

2.3.8 - How Do You Use "Application Specific Passwords"?

Generally you will need an Application Specific Password when you are setting up some 3rd party application that needs to access your Google Account. Applications that need to access Gmail or Picasa are common. These 3rd party applications don't know anything about 2-Step Verification and cannot send a verification code to your mobile phone. So, what happens?

For example, you are trying to set up your Apple "Mail" app on your iPad or iPhone to collect messages sent to your Gmail account. You have entered your correct Google Account password, but the app keeps telling you that you have used an incorrect password and it keeps asking you to enter the correct one. After you have entered your correct Google Account password a couple of times with no success, it will suddenly occur to you, as it did to me, that this app needs an Application Specific Password. Once again, apps that need Application Specific Passwords don't know that they do - they can't ask you to enter one so you have to figure that out for yourself.

Get out your printed list of Application Specific Passwords and enter one of them. You can enter any one of them. Cross off the one you use since you cannot use that one again. If everything works as it should, your Apple Mail app will now be happy and it will be able to sign-in to your Gmail account and collect your email.

2.3.9 - Revoking "Application Specific Passwords"

If your mobile phone is lost or stolen, Google recommends that you revoke your Application Specific Passwords and change the password for your Google Account. You can do this from a trusted computer. To revoke Application Specific Passwords, go to the page shown in the previous figure and click on the "[Revoke]" link next to each Application Specific Password you have used. You can get to this page by following this link:

https://accounts.google.com/IssuedAuthSubTokens

2.3.10 - Returning to Your Security Settings Page

You will probably need to return to your Account Security page several times. You can do this by going to:

https://www.google.com/settings/security

You can also bookmark this web page to make returning to it even easier.

The Main Features of the Nexus-7

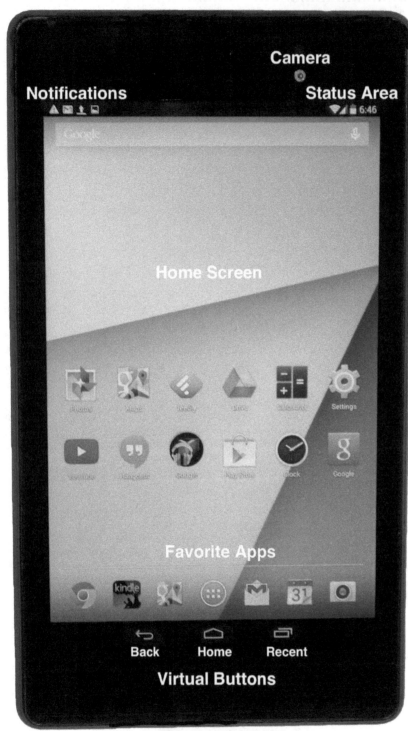

Camera

Notifications

Status Area

Power Button

Volume Button

Home Screen

Favorite Apps

Back   Home   Recent

Virtual Buttons

SIM Card Slot

Micro USB Port

3 - Getting Familiar with Nexus-7

3.1 - The Main Components of the Nexus-7

The figure on the previous page shows the main components of the Nexus-7.

3.1.1 - The Power Button

The Power button is located in the upper right corner of the Nexus-7. You will use this button to turn your Nexus-7 ON and OFF as well as to put it to sleep and to wake it from sleep.

To turn your Nexus-7 ON, press and hold the Power button until "Google" appears on the screen. Release the Power button and you will be entertained by colorful dancing balls while the Nexus-7 finishes starting up.

To turn the Nexus-7 OFF, press and hold the Power button until a menu appears in the center of the screen with an option to "Power Off". Touch the "Power Off" menu item and you will be asked to confirm that you really want to shut your Nexus-7 OFF. Touch "OK" and the Nexus-7 will turn itself OFF.

The Nexus-7 also has a power saving sleep mode. It enters this mode automatically when you haven't done anything for some period of time. You can also put the Nexus-7 to sleep by pressing the Power button briefly. Similarly, you wake the Nexus-7 from sleep by pressing the Power button briefly.

When the Nexus-7 wakes from sleep, it will display the "Lock Screen". Exactly what this looks like and what you have to do to unlock the Nexus-7 depends upon how you have set up your Nexus-7. This will be discussed in Section 4.5. In its factory fresh condition, the Nexus-7 will display a Lock Screen with a padlock icon surrounded by a white circle. Touch and drag the padlock icon away from the center of the circle to unlock the Nexus-7.

The Power button is also used in conjunction with the Volume button to take a screen shot should you want to take a picture of what's displayed on your screen. Hold down both the Power button and the Volume Down button at the same time until you hear a shutter sound and a picture of the screen will be stored in your "Photos" app.

3.1.2 - The Volume Button

For sound output, the Nexus-7 has speakers located at the bottom of the rear side and a headphone jack located just above the front-facing camera shown in the figure.

The Volume button is located just below the Power button on the right side of the Nexus-7. This is a rocker button. Push the lower portion of the rocker to lower the sound volume and push the upper portion to raise the sound volume.

3.1.3 - The SIM Card Slot

If you have a Nexus-7 with mobile data (LTE) capability, there will be a SIM card slot located near the bottom of the right edge of the device. You will also have received a SIM card and SIM card ejection tool along with your Nexus-7. Inserting and activating your SIM card will be explained in Section 4.6

3.1.4 - The micro USB Port

The micro USB port is located on the bottom of the Nexus-7. This is where you will plug in the charging cable that comes with the Nexus-7. You can also use this charging cable to connect your Nexus-7 to your personal computer to transfer files. You can also plug a micro USB OTG (On the Go) adaptor into this port which will allow you to connect external devices, such as an SD card reader, to your Nexus-7. This will be explained in Chapter 10 and Section 14.1.

3.1.5 - The Nexus-7 Cameras

The Nexus-7 has two cameras. The 1.2 mega-pixel, fixed focus, front facing camera is shown in Figure 3.1. There is also a 5 mega-pixel, auto focus, rear facing camera located on the back side just behind the front facing camera. Taking and managing photos will be discussed in Chapter 9

3.1.6 - The Touch Screen

The Touch Screen is the primary Nexus-7 input/output device. This is where all of the action occurs. You will interact with your Nexus-7 by using various touch gestures on the Touch screen. Touch screen gestures are explained in Section 3.2. The Nexus-7 will respond by displaying stuff on the Touch screen. The Touch Screen display is divided into several areas. Each area displays a different part of the Nexus-7 interface as explained in the following sections.

3.1.7 - The Notifications Area

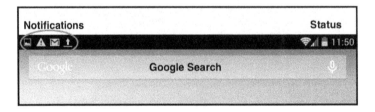

The Notifications Area is located in the upper left corner of the Touch Screen display. During normal operation, this area will display a row of small icons representing different types of Notifications that you will receive from time to time. For example, the third icon in the Notifications Area illustrated here looks like a small envelope with an "M" in it. This notifies me that I have received a new email message. It is also possible to reveal a more complete display of your current Notifications by "swiping" downward from the Notifications Area and I will discuss this more fully in Section 4.10. I will explain "swiping" and other Touch Screen gestures in Section 3.2.

3.1.8 - The Status Area

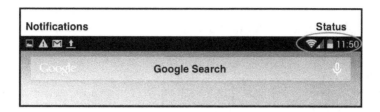

The Nexus-7 Status Area is located in the upper right corner of the Touch Screen display. During normal operation, this area will display a row of small icons depicting the current status of various Nexus-7 parameters such as WiFi and Mobile Data signal strengths, the battery charge level, and the current time. It is also possible to reveal a "Quick Settings" menu by swiping downward from the Status Area and I will discuss this in Section 4.10.

3.1.9 - The Nexus-7 "Virtual Buttons"

At the bottom of the Nexus-7 screen there is a row of three icons which I have labeled "Back", "Home", and "Recent". I call these "Virtual Buttons" because they are not actual physical buttons. They are normally displayed along the bottom edge of the Touch Screen display. However, some apps hide them while they are running. If they are not displayed, just touch the screen where they should be or swipe up from the bottom of the display and they will re-appear.

The basic function of these buttons is to "get me out of here". When you are finished with whatever you are doing, for instance when you have finished looking at the weather in Paris, and you want to get out of that app, touching one of these Virtual Buttons will do that for you.

The "Back" button normally takes you back to the previous screen. Sometimes this will be a previous screen in the current app, or it might take you back to the previous app. If you continue touching the Back button, you will eventually reach your Home Screen and you won't be able to go back any further.

The "Home" button will always take you back to your Home Screen. In the figure on page 28, the Home Screen is everything inside the black border around the display. Your Home Screen is divided into three parts. At the top is a standard Google Search Bar. At the bottom is a row of icons representing your favorite apps. These will always be displayed at the bottom of your Home Screen. I'll tell you how to set up this "Favorite Apps" display a little later. Normally, what is displayed between the Google Search Bar and the Favorite Apps icons is an array of other apps. I have shown a dozen apps in the figure. Because you may eventually accumulate a large collection of apps, the Nexus-7 provides you with five Home Screens. You switch between these pages by swiping left or right near the center of the display. You might also find other things displayed by swiping back and forth on the Home Screen. Sometimes there are recommendations for stuff to buy from the Google Play Store. Sometimes it might be quick links to your music collection. Just swipe back and forth and discover for yourself.

The "Recent" button will display a list of your recently used apps so that you can quickly switch between them. To open a recent app just touch its icon. To remove an app icon from this list and to quit that app just swipe its icon right or left out of the list.

3.1.10 - The Nexus-7 "All Apps" Button

At the bottom of every Nexus-7 Home Screen is an array of icons representing your six "Favorite" apps. But you may notice that there are actually seven icons - six that represent your Favorite Apps and a seventh icon that represents all of the apps that are installed on your Nexus-7. This "All Apps" icon is located right in the center of the Favorite Apps area. It looks like a circle with an array of small squares inside. Touching this icon will open a page with icons for all of the apps installed on your Nexus-7. You can select six of these apps to become your "Favorites". You can also populate your five Home Screens with dozens of apps that you use frequently but that do not qualify as one of your "Favorite Apps". I will explain how to do this in Section 4.7. But first we need to understand the various touch screen gestures that you will use to accomplish this.

3.2 - Getting Familiar with Touch Screen Gestures

Your main method for interacting with your Nexus-7 will be by using "gestures" on the Touch Screen. So it is important that you know the difference between "swipe" and "drag" for example.

But the most important thing that you need to know about the Touch Screen is that it is **not** pressure sensitive. It can't tell how hard you are pressing. If you press hard enough, you will break the glass screen. And the Nexus-7 will still ignore you. Just touch lightly. If it doesn't seem to work, try touching in a slightly different position. Don't press harder - it won't do any good.

OK, here are the main Touch Screen Gestures:

Touch - Touch the screen with one finger and remove it. Don't press!

Touch & Hold - This is also sometimes called "Long-Hold". Touch the screen with one finger and hold your finger on the screen without moving it. For example, if you touch the letter "e" on the Nexus-7 virtual keyboard and hold your finger on that letter, a small window will open allowing you to select an "e" with accent marks.

Touch, Hold & Drag - Touch the screen with one finger, hold for a second or two and then drag your finger across the screen without lifting it off the screen. This is how you will move app icons around your Home Screens.

Swipe - With your finger held just above the screen, begin sweeping your finger across the screen and touch the screen at the same time. You want to avoid touching the screen and then starting to move your finger - that would be a "touch, hold and drag" gesture. For example, you use the Swipe gesture to move between Home Screens.

Double Tap - Tap twice quickly with a single finger. This will generally zoom in or out of a page you are looking at. For example, tapping twice on a photo will zoom in for a closer view and tapping twice again will zoom back out. This is particularly useful if you are reading a web page where the "good stuff" - what you want to read - is contained in a column surrounded by advertisements and other stuff that you are not interested in reading. Just double tap anywhere in the column you want and it will (often) zoom in so that it occupies the entire screen while pushing the ads and other extraneous stuff off the screen. Double tap again to restore the full page view.

Pinch - Place two fingers on the screen at the same time. While holding your fingers on the screen, spreading them apart will enlarge the display, zooming in. Placing your two finger on the screen while holding them apart and then pinching them together while still touching the screen will squeeze the display smaller. For example, pinching on a photo that has been zoomed in will zoom that photo back out.

3.3 - Getting Familiar with Typing on Your Nexus-7

This is the default Nexus-7 keyboard. It will appear from the bottom of the screen whenever you touch a text entry area on the screen. For example when you need to enter your password or when you are typing an email message. You type on this virtual keyboard by touching the various keys. The letter keys, "qwerty", are pretty self explanatory, but some of the other keys may not be familiar so I will describe what they all do here. Starting at the upper-right corner and working around clockwise.

 Delete: Touching this key will delete the last character typed or the character to the left of the cursor if there is one. Holding on this key will delete characters rapidly.

 Return: Touching this key will end the current paragraph and start a new one. It will also act as an "enter" key when, for example, you have finished typing your password and want to "enter" it.

 Shift: Shifts between upper and lower case letters. Touching and holding will set caps-lock. Touching again will cancel caps-lock.

 Emoji: Switches to an Emoji keyboard where you can select from hundreds of Emoji symbols.

Hide the Keyboard: This symbol appears at the bottom of the screen when a keyboard is present. Touching it will dismiss and hide the keyboard.

 Dictate: Touching this key will cause the Nexus-7 to use speech-recognition to "type" what you speak. You have to say stuff like "period new paragraph" to insert punctuation.

 Numbers & Symbols: Touching this key will replace the qwerty keyboard with one that has numbers and a few special symbols as illustrated at the right. When this keyboard is displayed, the "Shift" keys are replaced with one that looks like this example at the left. Touching this symbols key will switch the keyboard to another one containing even more symbol keys as illustrated below at the right.

OK, that pretty much summarizes the various keys and keyboards. But there are a few other things to know about typing on the Nexus-7.

Typing Accented Letters: Foreign words often contain letters that have accent marks. You can type these accented letters on your Nexus-7, but there is a trick to doing it. If you touch&hold on a letter that has accented versions, a small pop-up menu will appear as illustrated at the right. Without lifting your finger off the screen, slide until you are touching the accented letter you want and then raise your finger. The accented letter will be typed for you.

Notice that this touch&hold is also a quick shortcut for typing numbers. Instead of switching to the numbers keyboard as described above, just touch and hold on one of the keys along the top edge of the keyboard, the "qwerty" row. Notice that these keys have numbers on them as well as the standard letters. So, touch and hold on the letter key that has the number you want to type, wait for the pop-up menu to appear and then slide to the number. Much quicker than switching keyboards.

Creating an Insertion Point: When you have typed some text but want to go back to correct or change something, you need a way to put an insertion point where you need to make those changes.

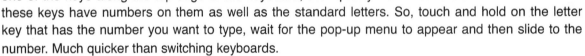

Just touch the screen where you want the insertion point to appear. It will look like this illustration. You can move this insertion point by touching and dragging the blue, pointed handle just below the insertion point. Touching the Delete key will delete the letter to the left of the insertion point. Typing will insert text to the right of the insertion point.

Selecting Text: To select text that you want to copy, edit, or delete, touch and hold somewhere in the text you want to select. The text you have touched will be highlighted in blue and two blue handles will appear at the two ends of the selected text. You can touch and drag these handles to expand or contract the selection.

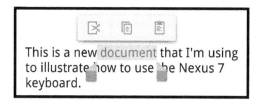

This is a new document that I'm using to illustrate how to use the Nexus 7 keyboard.

Cut, Copy, and Paste Text: When you have selected some text in this manner, a small menu will appear above the selected text as illustrated in the figure just above.

 The small icon at the left that looks like a sheet of paper with scissors cuts the selected text from your document and places it on a clip-board from which you can paste it somewhere else in your document. Touch this icon to cut text.

 This icon copies text from the selected area. The copied text is placed on a clip board as with cut, but in the copy case, the selected text remains it its original position in you document.

This "Paste" icon represents the clip board where your copied or cut text resides while you find somewhere to paste it back into your document. You can select some text and then touch this "Paste" icon in which case the pasted text will replace the text you selected. Or you can place an insertion point somewhere in your text and then touch the "Paste" icon. This will insert the pasted text into your document where you have placed the insertion point.

Using "Suggestions": When you start typing a word, your Nexus-7 will suggest possible words that you might be trying to type. Three of these suggestions will appear

above the keyboard as shown in this illustration. I have typed "the" and the Nexus-7 is suggesting that I might be trying to type "these". "them", or "their". The most likely suggestion "them" in this case, is the one in the middle. If one of these words is actually what you are trying to type, it can be much faster to just touch the proper word rather than to go on typing. Another advantage of this is that the suggested words are all spelled correctly.

Notice that the middle suggested word, "them" in the illustration above has three small dots below it. This indicates that there are more possible suggestions. Touching and holding on this middle word will pop up a menu with other suggestions as illustrated at the right.

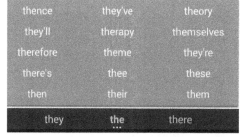

4 - Setting Up Your New Nexus-7

OK - at this point we have explored the main components of the Nexus-7 and how to interact with its controls and buttons. We can now go back and discuss starting up your new Nexus-7 for the first time.

4.1 - Charging the Nexus-7 Battery

Your Nexus-7 battery should be at least partially charged when you receive it, but it would be a good idea to charge it up before starting the initial setup process. The setup process could take a while and you don't want to run out of power half way through some procedure. You can charge your Nexus-7 battery while you read the rest of this chapter.

4.1.1 - Using the Nexus-7 Battery Charger

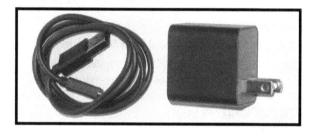

Your Nexus-7 comes with a wired battery charger. The USB end of the included cable plugs into the USB port on the charger. The micro-USB end of the included cable plugs into the micro-USB port on the bottom of the Nexus-7. Be careful, the micro-USB plug only goes in one way. If it seems difficult to insert the plug into the port, try turning the plug over. Don't force things else you might break it.

4.1.2 - Using the Nexus-7 Wireless Induction Charger

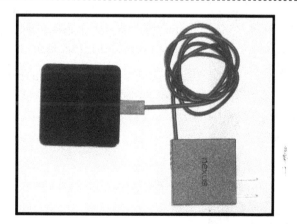

There is an optional, extra cost - approximately $50 - induction battery charger available from the Google Play Store for the Nexus-7. The induction charger plugs into a wall socket, but there is no cable that attaches it to the Nexus-7. All you have to do is place the Nexus-7, back-side down, onto the induction charger pad and the battery will begin charging. The bottom of the charger pad is slightly sticky so that it adheres to whatever you put in on. The Nexus-7 is held to the charger pad by the magnetic field generated by the charger. If you gently slide the Nexus-7 around on the charger pad, you will feel it "lock onto" the charger.

This is very convenient. I have adhered the inductive charger pad to the night-stand next to my bed. When I'm done reading for the night, I just put the Nexus-7 onto the charger and it is fully charged the next morning ready for a full day's use.

4.2 - Initial Setup of Your Nexus-7

Note: In order to set up your new Nexus-7, you must have a WiFi network available.

The first person to set up an account on a new Nexus-7 becomes the "Owner" of that device. The "Owner" has privilege to do stuff that the other users do not. Such as adding and deleting other users. So, if you plan to add other users to your Nexus-7, be sure that you do this initial setup process yourself.

To turn your Nexus-7 ON for the first time, press and hold the Power button until "Google" appears on the screen. Release the Power button and you will be entertained by colorful dancing balls while the Nexus-7 finishes starting up. This could take a while so be patient.

The first startup screen you see should look something like this. You can choose your preferred language by scrolling up or down with your finger where it says "English (United States). The text displayed by the Android OS will be in the language you select, but not all apps will agree with your selection. Some of them will display in English, or their native language, regardless of what you choose here.

After you have selected your preferred language, touch the forward facing triangle to go to the next screen.

All models of the Nexus-7 can connect to the internet via a WiFi network. Some models, the "LTE" models, can also connect via a mobile phone network. Generally this is done only if a WiFi network is not available.

If you didn't buy the mobile data capable LTE model of the Nexus-7, you won't see this screen and you can just skip to the next screen below.

If you have the mobile data (LTE) model of the Nexus-7, you will be asked to insert the SIM card that came with your Nexus-7 at this point. I would recommend that you choose "Skip" at this point. Setting up the Nexus-7 for the first time is a little complex and the SIM card setup, which is also complex, can be done at a later time. Personally, I found trying to do both at the same time to be confusing.

At this point, your Nexus-7 will search for and display all of the WiFi networks it can find in your area. Hopefully, one of these will be your network. If you have a WiFi router that does not broadcast its network name, then you will not see it in this list. In this case you should touch "Other Network" near the bottom of the screen and type in your network name (SSID).

If you do see the name of your network in the list, just touch it and that will take you to the next screen.

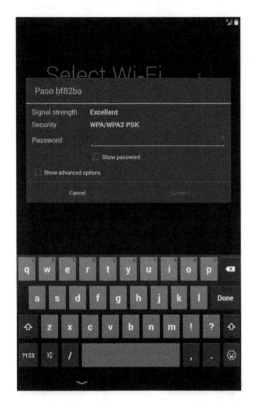

If you have not set a password for your WiFi network, shame on you. You are asking for trouble. Stop right now and go set up a password protected WiFi network before proceeding here. I'll wait.

OK, so now we are all on this screen where you will enter the password for your encrypted WiFi network. I find that checking (touching) the box labeled "Show Password" is a great help in avoiding typing errors. When you have entered your password, touch "Connect". After a brief pause while your Nexus-7 connects to your WiFi network you will be taken to the next screen.

If you have followed my advice in Chapter 2 and set up your Google Account using your personal computer, then you can answer "Yes" here and proceed to the next screen.

If you have not set up a Google Account yet, you can do that here by touching "No". This will take you through a very abbreviated setup process which will result in a Google Account "Lite". You will still have to visit your account using a personal computer in order to configure many of the account settings, particularly the security settings, that are not included in this simplified set up process.

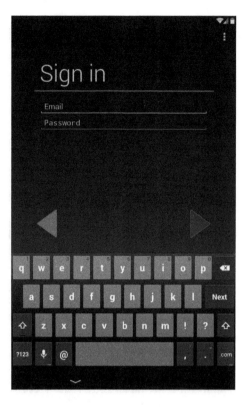

This is where you sign-in to your Google Account. You don't have to type your full email address, just the part that comes before the "@". Google is clever enough to figure out that if you type "JoeBlow" your full address is "JoeBlow@gmail.com". Google account names are not case sensitive so that JoeBlow is the same as joeblow.

When you have entered your account name and password, touch the forward facing triangle to take you to the next screen.

If you have set up "2 Step Verification" (also known as "2 factor authentication") for your account, you will see this screen. Don't panic. All it means is that you will now have to supply the verification code in addition to your user name and password. Just touch "Next" to go to the screen where you can do that.

If you have not set up "2-Step Verification" you should have. It will make your life a little more complicated, but it will also make your Google Account a lot more secure. I explain how it works and how to set it up in Section 2.3.

If you have not set up "2-Step Verification", you will not see this screen and you can skip ahead to the "Google Services" screen 3 pages ahead.

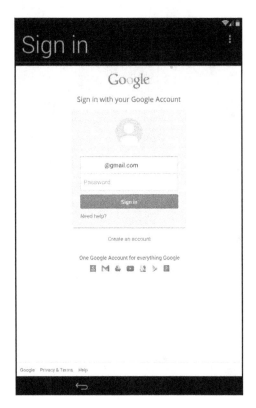

Here you get to sign-in again. Google will remember the account name that you entered previously, but you will have to enter your account password once again.

After entering your password, touching "Sign In" will take you to the next screen.

This is where you will enter the 6-digit verification code from your mobile phone.

If you have set up 2-Step Verification to deliver your 6-digit verification code via text message or via voice message to your mobile phone, you should receive it shortly. If you have chosen to use Google Authenticator on your mobile phone, this is the time to launch that app. Google Authenticator will generate a 6-digit verification code that will be valid for 1 minute. Refer back to Section 2.3.6 to refresh your memory about Google Authenticator and how to use it.

If you can't get a 6-digit verification code from your mobile phone for some reason, then this is the time to find those "Backup Codes" you printed out when you set up 2-Step Verification. You did save those Backup Codes didn't you?

You will only have to do this 2-Step Verification process once on your Nexus-7. Afterwards your user name and password will be all you need enter.

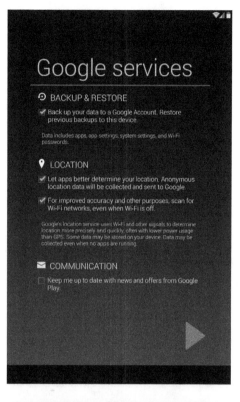

This is where you can "opt-out" of a few Google Services. Personally I don't see any reason to opt-out of the "Backup & Restore" nor of the "Location" services, but you may feel differently.

I have opted-out of the "Communication" offer to keep me informed of news and offers from Google, but , once again, you may feel differently.

Once you have made your choices, touch the forward facing triangle to move on to the next screen.

Your name should already be filled in on this screen, so, unless you want to change it, just touch the forward facing triangle to move on to the next screen.

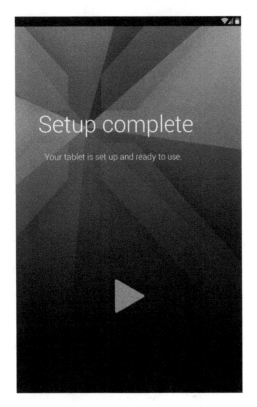

That's it. You're done with the initial setup of your Nexus-7. Touching the forward facing triangle on this screen will take you to your Home Page where you can start using your Nexus-7.

If you have a mobile data ("LTE") model of the Nexus-7, Section 4.6 will explain how to install and activate the SIM card that came with it.

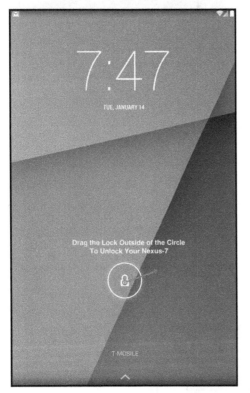

There is one other thing you need to know before we leave this section. If you turn your Nexus-7 OFF or if it goes to "sleep", then when you turn it back ON again or wake it up, you will see this Lock Screen.

This is the Nexus-7 default Lock Screen. When you turn the Nexus-7 ON it will be locked and this screen will be displayed. If you don't do anything for some settable length of time, the device will lock itself and this screen will be displayed.

There are several different ways to Lock the Nexus-7, each with its own Lock Screen. I will discuss changing your Lock Screen in Section 4.5. However, until you change it, this will be the Lock Screen.

To Unlock this default Lock Screen, just drag the little lock icon in any direction out of the circle.

4.3 - Adding and Deleting Other Users on Your Nexus-7

4.3.1 - Adding Another User to Your Nexus-7

The first person to set up an account on a new Nexus-7 becomes the "Owner" of that device. The "Owner" has privilege to do stuff that the other users do not. Such as adding and deleting other users. The Nexus-7 can support up to 8 different users. Each user will have their own "space" on the Nexus-7. All documents, photos, music, etc will be owned by that user and none of the other users will be able to access that user's stuff.

Only the Owner can add a new user. So the first thing to do is to be sure that you are signed-in as the Owner. To add a new user, start by swiping downward from the upper-right corner of the screen to reveal the "Quick Settings" menu, a portion of which looks like this. Touch the "Settings", gear shaped, icon to open the full settings menu.

In order to save space, I have "edited" the full Settings Menu to look like this. In reality, the "Users" menu item is quite a way down the menu. Just look down the menu and find the "Users" item and touch it.

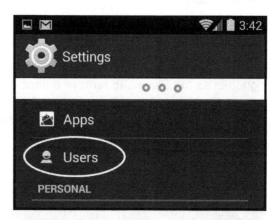

That will open a listing of all the current users and the last item in that list will be "Add User or Profile". Touch that item.

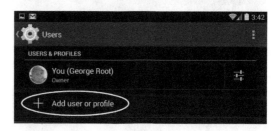

That opens this dialog where you can choose whether you want to add a new user or restrict the profile of an existing user. If you are adding an underage user, you might want to come back and restrict the type of apps and web content they can access. If you do this, be sure to also add a PIN to your Lock Screen else the restricted user can simply sign-in as you and remove the restrictions.

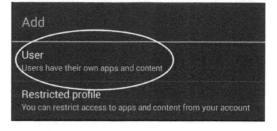

Google then displays this informational panel telling you some of the things to be aware of when you add a new user. This is your last chance to "Cancel".

If you decide to proceed, just touch the "OK". You will be asked whether you want to add the new user now or later.

Select "Now" and you will be taken back to the "Welcome" screen at the beginning of the process for adding the first user. This process is described in Section 4.2. Go through the same process now for the new user you want to add. If the new user already has a Google Account, this process will be fast and easy. Just provide the new user's account name and password. You will also be given the opportunity to sign up for a Google Wallet account if the new user doesn't already have one. A Google Wallet account, including a credit card number, is required to buy music, apps, and other stuff from the Google Pay Store. You might want to consider if this is something you want to do if you are adding an underage user.

4.3.2 - Removing a User from Your Nexus-7

Only the "Owner" of a Nexus-7 can remove users. So the first thing to do is to be sure that you are signed-in as the Owner. To remove a user, start by swiping downward from the upper-right corner of the screen to reveal the "Quick Settings" menu. Touch the "Settings", gear shaped, icon to open the full settings menu. Look down this menu and find the "Users" item and touch it.That will open a listing of all the current users. I have not illustrated these steps because they are the same as those shown in the previous section.

Find the User you want to remove from your Nexus-7 in the list of users. To the right of that user's name will be a trash-can icon shown outlined in this figure. Touch that icon. That will take you to the next figure where you have to confirm that you really do want to remove this user and all of this user's stuff from your Nexus-7.

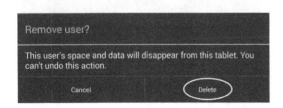

Touch "Delete" to remove the User.

4.4 - Signing-In and Signing-Out When There Are Multiple Users

If you are the only user of your Nexus-7 you don't have to sign-in nor sign-out. But if there are multiple users, you do have to sign-out of your account before a different user can sign-in. Only one user can be signed-in at a time.

4.4.1 - Signing-In to a Nexus-7 with Multiple Users

When there is more than one user of a Nexus-7, the Lock Screen will display a row of user photos and names along the lower edge of the screen. Just touch your photo to sign-in. You then will have to unlock the Lock Screen.

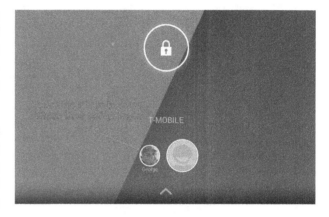

If you want to restrict access to different user accounts on the Nexus-7 then you should set the Lock Screen to require at least a PIN to unlock the screen. Setting the different ways to lock and unlock the Lock Screen is described in Section 4.5.

4.4.2 - Signing-Out of a Nexus-7 with Multiple Users

Signing-out of your account on a Nexus-7 with multiple users is easy. Just swipe downward from the upper-right corner of the screen to display the "Quick Settings" menu. Your photo, the one that you have associated with your Google Account, will be shown in the upper-left corner as illustrated here. The "photo" in this illustration is the one you will be

assigned if you don't supply one of your own. Just touch this photo and you will be signed-out of your account and taken back to the Lock Screen.

4.5 - Managing Your Nexus-7 Lock Screen

There are 5 different ways to lock and unlock your Lock Screen. Each user can choose a different locking/unlocking method.

To get started choosing the method you want to use to unlock your Lock Screen, swipe downward starting in the upper-right corner of the screen to reveal the "Quick Settings" menu. Touch the gear shaped "Settings" item to reveal the complete Settings Menu. Look down the list of Settings. Just below the Personal heading, touch "Security".

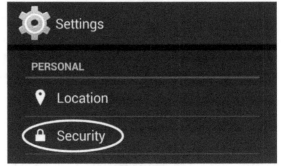

Look down the list that opens and touch "Screen Lock". Just below the "Screen Lock" item shown outlined in the figure, is the name of the current locking method - "Slide" in this case.

Touching "Screen Lock" will reveal a list of the five possible locking methods available on the Nexus-7. Each of these methods will be discussed in the following sections.

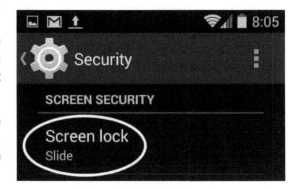

4.5.1 - Using "Slide" to Unlock the Nexus-7 Lock Screen

"Slide" is the least secure method for locking your Nexus-7. This is the default screen lock and it is the method we have been using so far in this book. All that is required to unlock the Lock Screen using "Slide" is to touch the padlock icon in the center of the screen and drag it outside the circle. This method provides no security at all since anyone can slide the lock.

4.5.2 - Using "Face Unlock" to Unlock the Nexus-7 Lock Screen

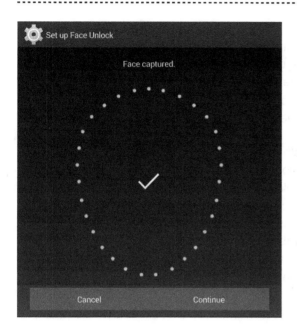

"Face Unlock" is the easiest and least secure method of unlocking your Nexus-7. It is easy because all you have to do is look at the screen and, in theory, the Nexus-7 will recognize you and unlock itself. It is the least secure method because it is likely that it will recognize someone else's face and unlock the screen for them too. Or, even more likely it won't recognize you.

Because Face Unlock is not 100% accurate, the Nexus-7 provides a backup method to use when face recognition fails. You can choose to use a Pattern or a PIN as backup. I would skip Face Unlock and go directly with a PIN.

4.5.3 - Using a "Pattern" to Unlock the Nexus-7 Lock Screen

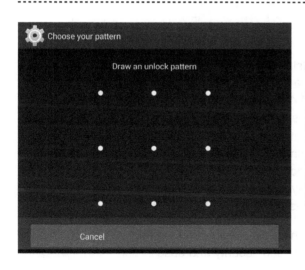

"Pattern" locking allows you to draw a simple pattern, connecting the dots on the screen, to unlock the Lock Screen. This method is more secure than Face Unlock, but less so than PIN or Password. Is it easier to remember and to duplicate a pattern than a PIN? I don't think so, but you might like to try this method and see for yourself.

4.5.4 - Using a "PIN" to Unlock the Nexus-7 Lock Screen

With "PIN" unlocking you choose a Personal Identification Number (PIN) of 4 or more digits as the unlock code for your Lock Screen. This is generally quite secure, especially so if you choose more than 4 digits, and you don't choose something too obvious like 1-2-3-4 or 5-5-5-5. It is also fairly simple and fast to use. This is the method I use. With a 7 digit PIN. There are 10 million possible combinations. That pretty much precludes trial and error PIN breaking. You can also combine the Pattern and PIN methods by choosing your PIN based on a pattern on the number pad. It is easier to reproduce that PIN accurately than it would be to reproduce the pattern using the Pattern method.

4.5.5 - Using a "Password" to Unlock the Nexus-7 Lock Screen

Using a password is the most secure way to lock the Lock Screen. You can choose any combination of 4 or more letters and numbers. Once again, this is secure provided you don't use a weak password that is too easy to guess, like "password" or your name. For this extra security, you pay the price of added complexity since you have to deal with a full keyboard making it more difficult to enter your Password every time you unlock your Lock Screen.

I think that using PIN locking is a good tradeoff between security and ease of use.

4.5.6 - Adding Owner Info to the Nexus-7 Lock Screen

It is possible to display information on your Nexus-7 Lock Screen. For example, you might like to put your name and phone number on the Lock Screen so that, if someone finds your lost Nexus-7, they will be able to contact you to return it. Or not.

To add owner information to your Lock Screen, start by swiping downward from the upper-right corner of the screen to reveal the "Quick Settings" menu. Touch the "Settings", gear shaped, icon to open the full settings menu. Look down this menu and find the "Users" item and touch it. That will open a listing of all the current users. I have not illustrated these steps because they are the same as those we have used several times before.

The first user in the list of users will be the "Owner" of the Nexus-7 and to the right of that user's name will be an icon that looks something like an abacus shown outlined in this figure. Touch that icon.

On this screen you can type whatever information you want to display on your Lock Screen. Remember that anyone who finds your Nexus-7 will be able to see this information. So you may not want to put your entire address here. I just typed my name and phone number. That way someone who finds my Nexus-7 can call me to return it. If you would be willing to pay a reward for the return, you might mention that here as well. It might increase the likelihood of getting it back.

What you type will scroll across the Lock Screen in a single line of text so you don't have to worry about formatting what you type. You can also type more than will fit on the width of the Lock Screen since your text will scroll across the screen.

4.6 - Setting Up Your Nexus-7 SIM Card

Note: If you did not purchase a mobile data ("LTE") model of the Nexus-7, you can skip this section.
Note: You must have adequate mobile network signal strength to complete this setup.

There are two mobile data providers for the Nexus-7 in the US: AT&T and T-Mobile. There are many other possible providers in other countries. So, it will not be possible for me to give detailed instructions for every possible mobile data provider. However, you will have received detailed instructions from your provider along with the SIM card for your Nexus-7. I will give some examples from the T-Mobile activation process but yours may differ slightly.

4.6.1 - Disabling WiFi

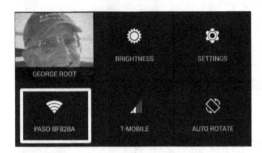

Before you can set up your SIM card, you will have to disable WiFi on your Nexus-7 in order to force the Nexus-7 to use mobile data to connect with your provider's website. To do this you need to access the Nexus-7 "Quick Settings" illustrated in this figure. To reveal these Quick Settings I find it easiest to start just above the upper-right corner of the screen and swipe down toward the lower left corner. You can actually swipe downward starting anywhere above the right half of the screen. The WiFi settings are shown outlined with a white rectangle in this figure. The name of your WiFi network will be shown. To turn WiFi OFF, first touch the WiFi icon near the center of the outlined rectangle.

Touching the WiFi icon near the center of the outlined rectangle will reveal this panel with an ON/OFF switch. Touch "ON" and drag the switch left to the "OFF" position.

Now, turn your Nexus-7 itself OFF by holding the Power Button in until this panel is displayed near the center of the screen. Touch "Power OFF" and then confirm that you want to turn the power OFF on the next screen and your Nexus-7 will power down.

Now, with the power OFF you can insert the SIM card.

4.6.2 - Inserting Your SIM Card into the Nexus-7

Google provides this helpful little figure showing how to insert your SIM card into the Nexus-7. The SIM card slot is located at the bottom of the right edge of the Nexus-7. There is a SIM card carrier in this slot with a small hole near the bottom edge of the carrier. Insert the SIM carrier ejector tool that came with your Nexus-7 into that little hole and push it in carefully but with enough force to pop the carrier out of the slot. The carrier will only pop out a short distance. You can pull the carrier completely out of the Nexus-7 slot with your fingernails.

The SIM card from T-Mobile is shown in this figure. The actual SIM card itself is the little chip shown outlined in the figure. Just pop the small SIM card out of the larger plastic card and put it into the carrier with the contacts facing upward. You can now slide the SIM card along with its carrier back into the SIM card slot in your Nexus-7.

To replace or upgrade your current SIM card, you can visit www.t-mobile.com/sim or call 1.877.234.4299

4.6.3 - Activating Your SIM Card

Turn your Nexus-7 back ON by holding in the Power Button until you see the word "Google" appear on the screen. You can then release the Power Button and watch the bouncing balls while the Nexus-7 starts up.

 At this point the Chrome Browser may start up automatically. If it doesn't, touch the "All Apps" icon on your Home Screen (see Section 3.1.10) and find the Chrome icon and touch it. Chrome will launch and go to your mobile data provider's website automatically.

At this point in the SIM card activation process, the details of what you do will vary depending upon which mobile data provider you have. I will give some examples from the T-Mobile activation process. Hopefully your process will be similar.

There are basically two different types of mobile data plans offered by carriers:

1) Pre-Paid or Pay-As-You-Go plans where you don't have a fixed term contract with the provider. You just pay for data as you use it.

2) Post-Paid or "contract" plans where you commit yourself to make monthly payments for a fixed duration, typically 2 years, regardless of whether or not you actually use any data during that period.

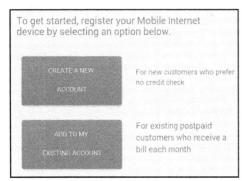

To get started, register your Mobile Internet device by selecting an option below.

CREATE A NEW ACCOUNT — For new customers who prefer no credit check

ADD TO MY EXISTING ACCOUNT — For existing postpaid customers who receive a bill each month

This figure from T-Mobile is somewhat dyslexic. The buttons on the left imply that you are choosing whether to create a new account or to add your Nexus-7 to a contract plan that you already have with T-Mobile. But the text next to the buttons says that you are choosing between a pre-paid or a monthly contract data plan. I would go with the labels on the buttons. I touched the "Create a New Account" button and that process later allowed me to choose a pre-paid or monthly contract plan.

The plans that you have available to you will depend upon your provider and when you sign up. As this is being written, T-Mobile is offering 200 MB of free mobile data per month for life. Although 200 MB is a small amount of data, "free" is a powerful inducement. That's why I bought the T-Mobile version of the Nexus-7.

I will mention at this point that the T-Mobile version of the Nexus-7 is "unlocked". This means that you can later choose to switch to AT&T, or any other GSM mobile data provider by simply buying a SIM card from them and activating it in your Nexus-7. This is particularly useful if you travel to Europe, or anywhere else in the world where they use the GSM mobile data system (read anywhere in the world except the US). You can simply buy a pre-paid SIM card from some local mobile data provider and activate it in your Nexus-7. This will be considerably less expensive than "roaming" with your US based SIM card.

During the account creation process you will have to provide personal information such as your name, address, email address, and phone number. T-Mobile will also ask for your birth date. If you don't feel comfortable giving this information, as I don't, just create a birth date close to your true one.

I should also mention that you will devise a password to protect your T-Mobile account. T-Mobile says that this password must contain at least 1 of each of the following: lower case letter, upper case letter, number, and special character. What T-Mobile doesn't say is that they don't allow any actual words to be used. So, just choose a random combination of every type of character on the keyboard.

At the end of the account creation process, you be given a "Device ID". This is actually the phone number, including area code, that has been assigned to your Nexus-7. Write this number down and keep it in case you have to contact your mobile data provider for any reason. They will want this Device ID.

At this point you should have mobile data available. But you want to go back and re-enable WiFi data. Your Nexus-7 will always use WiFi data if it is available. Only if no WiFi is available will the Nexus-7 use mobile data.

To re-enable WiFi data, go back to Section 4.6.1 and follow those instructions except that you will be turning the WiFi switch to the ON position.

4.6.4 - Monitoring and Limiting Mobile Data Usage

If you have selected a mobile data plan with a fixed data allocation each month, you will want to monitor and perhaps limit your mobile data usage to be sure you don't run over your data allocation.

To monitor and limit your mobile data usage, start by swiping downward from the upper-right corner of the screen to reveal the "Quick Settings" menu. Touch the "Settings", gear shaped, icon to open the full settings menu. Look down this menu and find the "Data Usage" item and touch it. I have not illustrated these steps because they are the same as those we have used several times before.

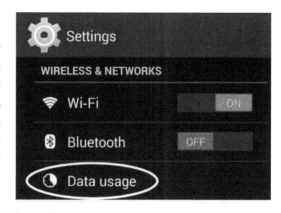

Touching "Date Usage" will open a screen with a lot of information on it. A list of apps and how much data they have used during your current billing period runs further down the screen than I have shown here.

At the top of this screen is where you can turn mobile data use OFF to prevent any usage of your allocation. Just touch "ON" and drag your finger to the left to the "OFF" position.

If you want to limit the amount of mobile data you use during each billing period, touch the check box labeled "1" in this figure to set a mobile data limit for each billing period.

Next touch the "Data Usage Cycle" item that I have labelled "2" in this figure.

That will bring up this screen where you can set the date of each month when your billing cycle ends. The Nexus-7 will keep track of how much data you use during each billing cycle and report it just below the graph in the previous figure..

You can also limit the amount of data you use each billing period. Go back to the previous figure and notice the two horizontal lines that end with dots (handles) I have labeled "3" in that figure. You can drag these "handles" up and down to set a limit on data used and a level where you will get a warning that you are approaching your data limit. So, in this example, I have limited myself to 200 MB per month with a warning set at 150MB.

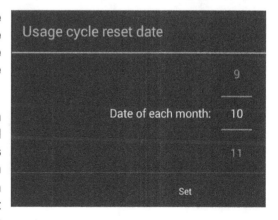

4.6.5 - Reducing Chrome Browser Data Usage

Android 32 introduced a new service that reduces the amount of data downloaded by the Chrome Browser on the Nexus-7. This makes your browsing faster and at the same time may save you on data costs. When you request a web page, Google examines that page and applies lossless compression to reduce the amount of data that will be sent to your Chrome Browser. In the process, it also examines the contents of the page to detect malicious content. Win-win. SSL (encrypted) and "Incognito" pages are not processed in this way.

By default, this service is turned OFF. To enable it on your Nexus-7 follow these steps.

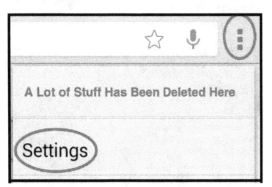

Launch the Chrome Browser on your Nexus-7. In the upper-right corner of the Chrome window is an icon that looks like three small squares in a vertical array. This is the standard Android icon for indicating a menu. Touch the three-square icon and a menu will drop down as illustrated in this figure. Near the bottom of this menu is an item labeled "Settings". Touch that and the Chrome Settings window will open as illustrated in the next figure.

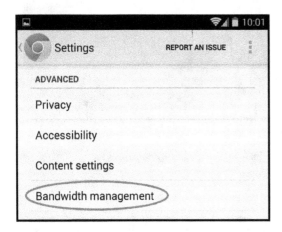

Near the bottom of the Chrome Browser Settings menu is an item "Bandwidth Management". Touch that and a window such as that illustrated in the next figure will open.

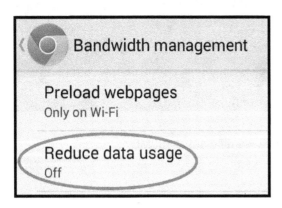

Touch "Reduce Data Usage" to open a page like the one on the next page.

When you first see this page, the switch in the upper-right corner will be "OFF". Just touch-hold and slide that switch to the right to turn data usage reduction ON as I have done here.

The graph shows how much data usage has been reduced. In this example, my data usage has been reduced by 37% in just the past few hours since I turned this service ON.

This data reduction service applies to both WiFi and mobile data. I have included it here in the section discussing mobile data because it is more likely to be of interest to people trying to reduce their mobile data charges. All of the 37% reduction in data illustrated in this figure has occurred while I have been using a WiFi connection.

4.7 - Setting Up Your Home Screens and Favorite Apps Bar

Your Nexus-7 comes with dozens of apps already installed. You will also most likely buy dozens more from the Google Play Store. Eventually you will have a hard time finding the app you are looking for. So, Google has provided the Nexus-7 with two ways to simplify your search: Home Screens and the Favorite Apps Bar. You can choose which apps are displayed in each of these locations. Your Favorite Apps Bar should contain the six apps that you use most frequently. Your Home Screens should contain other apps that you use frequently, but not frequently enough to warrant "Favorite" status.

4.7.1 - Adding Apps to Your Home Screens

Your Nexus-7 has five Home Screens. The center one is the default Home Screen. It is the one you will go to when you touch the Home Screen button (the little house) at the bottom of the screen. You move between these five Home Screens by swiping left or right. So, if the Home Screens were numbered (which they are not), the leftmost screen would be #1, the middle one (the default Home Screen) would be #3 and the rightmost screen would be #5. In its factory fresh condition, Home Screen #4 has been assigned to display your "Library". This contains stuff you have purchased from the Google Play Store. Home Screen #5 has been taken over by Google to advertise stuff available from the Google Play Store. You can remove the contents of these two screens so that all five screens are available for your use. This is explained in Section 4.7.2. Your five Home Screens can contain apps or "Widgets" which I will explain in Section 4.7.4.

When you first start up your new Nexus-7, the bottom of your Home Screen looks something like this:

I have only shown the bottom of the screen to save space. The Home Screen above the portion shown in this figure will be empty. If you look closely at the white line just above your Favorites Bar, you will see that a short portion of this line is slightly wider than the rest of the line. This wide portion indicates which of the five Home Screens you are currently looking at. In this example, we are looking at the fourth Home Screen. This indicator only appears when you are swiping between Home Screens. It then fades away.

So, how do you put apps on your Home Screen? First, if you are not on the Home Screen you want to add an app to, then touch the virtual "Home" button - the one that looks like a little house at the bottom of any screen and swipe left or right until you get to your desired Home Screen. Next, touch the "All Apps" button just above the Home button. It's the one with six little squares in it.

Touching the "All Apps" button will open a screen containing icons for all of the apps that are installed on your Nexus-7. It will look something like this. If you swipe across this screen from right to left, more pages of apps will be revealed. If you continue swiping after the last page of apps, you will reveal page after page of "Widgets". I'll discuss "Widgets" in a while. On this "All Apps" screen, find the icon for an app that you will use frequently enough to add it to one of your Home Screens. Then just touch and hold your finger on that icon. Don't move your finger, just hold it there. After a second or two, the "All Apps" screen will disappear and you will still have your finger on the icon for your chosen app except that now your finger will be on your Home Screen. At this point you can drag the app icon to any part of the Home Screen and drop it there by lifting your finger off the screen. The icon will snap to the closest empty spot on the screen.

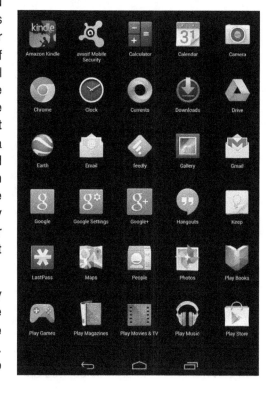

You can "nudge" other app icons out of the way by slowly dragging the one you are moving toward the one you are trying to nudge. If the app icon moves out of the way, drop the one you are moving onto the empty spot. If you drop the icon you are moving onto another app icon, you will create a folder containing both apps.

You can create folders to help organize your apps. To do this, touch-hold-and-drag the icon for one app onto the icon for another app. Hold a second and a black circle will appear around the 'bottom' icon. Drop the icon you are moving inside this circle and a folder containing both apps will be created.

You can name this folder by touching the folder and then touching the default name "Unnamed Folder". An insertion point will appear along with a keyboard. Type the new folder name and then touch "Done"

To select an app that is inside a folder, first touch the folder which will open it as illustrated here and then touch the icon for the app you want. To move an app out of a folder, just touch-hold-and-drag its icon out of the folder. If there is only a single app left in the folder, the folder itself will be destroyed.

4.7.2 - Removing Apps from Your Home Screens

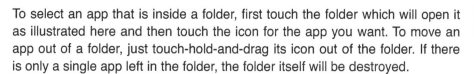

Actually, your Home Screens contain "short cuts" or "pointers" to your frequently used apps. The apps themselves stay on the "All Apps" Screen. So, removing an app from your Home Screen doesn't delete it from your Nexus-7. Removing apps from your Home Screens is easy. Touch-and-Hold the icon for the app you want to remove. After a second or two a label will appear at the top of the screen saying "X Remove". Just drag the app to this label and it will be eliminated from the Home Screen.

4.7.3 - Adding Apps to Your Favorites Bar

Adding apps to your Favorites Bar works pretty much the same as adding them to your Home Screen. The main difference is that your Favorites Bar can only hold icons for your six most favorite apps. So, if you already have six apps in your Favorites Bar, you will have to remove one of them to make space for a different "Favorite".

To remove an app from your Favorites Bar, touch-hold-and-drag the icon upward out of the Favorites Bar. You can then drop it somewhere on your Home Screen, or you can continue dragging it upward onto the "X Remove" label to remove it entirely.

As with your Home Screens, you can also create folders of apps in your Favorites Bar. Drag one app onto another app that is already in the Favorites Bar and a folder will be created containing both apps. Touch this folder and it will "pop out" of the Favorites Bar onto the Home Screen from where you can name the folder or select one app from inside the folder.

4.7.4 - Adding Widgets to Your Home Screens

Widgets are actually apps that run on your Home Screen. You don't have to launch them, they are always there and running. For example I have a widget that shows me a few of the most recent messages in my Gmail Inbox. I don't have to launch Gmail itself. The Widget keeps itself updated. If I want to read the entire message all I have to do is touch the summary in the Inbox Widget. Or, I can compose a new email message by touching the "envelope" icon in the upper-right corner of the Widget. Very handy.

This figure illustrates the Gmail Inbox Widget on the left and a Google Calendar Widget that I have added to my Home Screen on the right. If I touch the Calendar Event "Dinner with Bill & Mary", that will launch the Calendar app and take me to that Event.

There are several Widgets already on your Nexus-7. If you swipe from right to left on the "All Apps" screen, you will come to pages of Widgets that you can install on one of your Home Screens. You can also buy apps and Widgets from the Google Play Store which I will discuss shortly.

Widgets can be resized. To resize a Widget, touch & hold until small white "handles" appear at the corners and centers of the sides of the widget. Then just drag one of these handles to resize.

4.7.5 - Adding Webpage Links to Your Home Screens

Android 32 has introduced a new feature making it possible to add an icon to your Home Screen that represents a link to a webpage. Touching this icon will launch the Chrome Browser and open that webpage.

 To get started, launch the Chrome Browser on your Nexus-7 and navigate to some webpage that you would like to revisit frequently. I have used the "Android Central" webpage for this illustration.

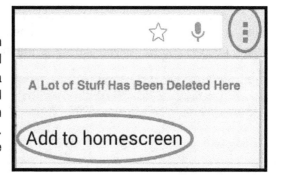

In the upper-right corner of the Chrome window is an icon that looks like three small squares in a vertical array. This is the standard Android icon for indicating a menu. Touch the three-square icon and a menu will drop down as illustrated in this figure. Near the bottom of this menu is an item labeled "Add to Home Screen". Touch that and an icon will be added to your Home Screen as illustrated below.

This is the "Android Central" link that has been added to my Home Screen. Touching this icon will launch the Chrome Browser and open the Android Central webpage. It is sort of like a bookmark on your Home Screen.

4.8 - Buying Stuff from the Google Play Store

 "Google Play" is actually two stores. On one you can buy "digital" stuff: apps, widgets, ebooks, music, videos, magazines. On the other Google Play Store, you can buy hardware - actual devices and accessories. For example, I bought my Nexus-7 from the Google Play Store. You will find this icon for the "Play Store" on your Nexus-7. Touching this icon will take you to the "digital" store where you can buy stuff to download to your Nexus-7. This is where you will buy more apps to install on your Nexus-7. I will discuss this process in the next section.

To get to the Google Play Device Store, you will have to use your Chrome web browser. Launch Chrome and go to this website: https://play.google.com/store/devices . If you think you might be coming back to the device store frequently, you might want to bookmark it, or even add a Home Screen Link to one of your Home Pages as explained in Section 4.7.5.

4.8.1 - Buying Apps from the Google Play Store

Start by touching the Play Store icon on one of your Home Pages. That will take you to the store site where you will see something like this at the top of the page:

 Touching one of these icons will take you to pages where you can buy "APPS", "GAMES", and so forth. Since we want to buy an app, touch the "APPS" icon. That will take you to a catalog of apps where you can browse or search for an app. If you know the name or a keyword associated with the app you are looking for, just touch the "magnifying glass" icon shown in the upper-right corner of the figure just above, type in your keyword and touch the magnifying glass to start the search. You can also browse for an app in categories such as "Top Free Apps", "Top Paid Apps", "Top New Apps" and so forth. Once you find an app that you might like, touch its icon and that will take you to a page devoted to that app.

 For example, here's a portion of the top of the page for a popular app called "SwiftKey". There is a lot more information on app pages than what I have shown here. Be sure to read any reviews and to also pay attention to how many people have downloaded and how many have rated the app.

Android apps are not as carefully curated as those for iOS devices. Google does remove apps that contain malicious code from the Play Store, but that is only after they have been available on the store for some time. It is possible for you to install a malicious app on your Nexus-7 without knowing it. That's why you need to pay attention to other user reviews and to the number of downloads that have been made. For example, SwiftKeys has been installed on over 1 million devices and has been rated by 350,000 people. If it were malicious, that would probably have been discovered by now.

Just to emphasize the fact that some apps may contain malicious code, Google warns you that the app you are about to install on your Nexus-7 is asking for permission to interact with components of your device. It lists the permissions the app is asking for. You can only accept or deny all of these. If you deny, the app will not be installed. You should only accept these permissions if you are confident that the app is not malicious. I will discuss the use of anti-virus software a little later. If you decide to go ahead with the installation of this app on your Nexus-7, touch the "Accept" button.

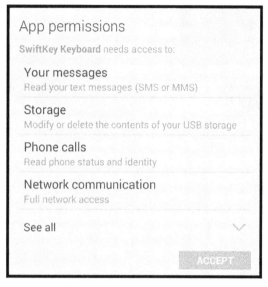

If you have accepted the permissions requested by the app, you will be taken through a series of pages where you will decide how to pay for it.

There are two primary ways to pay for stuff on the Google Play Store. You can enter a credit card number each time you make a purchase, or you can open a Google Wallet Account. This is the page where you would enter your credit card information.

If you have a Google Wallet Account, this is the page you will see when it comes to paying for your purchase. The colorful squiggle shown outlined in this figure is the symbol for Google Wallet. I will discuss Google Wallet further in the next section.

When you touch "BUY" on a Google Wallet payment page, this "Confirm Password" page will open. This requires you to type in your Account password again. You can tell Google not to ask again by touching the checkbox outlined in the figure, but that will allow anyone to make unlimited purchases using your Google Wallet Account - think of your 8 year old son or daughter. Probably not a good idea.

After you have completed your purchase of the app, it will be downloaded and installed on your Nexus-7. New apps will appear in your "All Apps" page and will also be added to your Home Screen. In addition, the app's page in the Google Play Store will change as illustrated in this figure. Instead of giving the price of the app, you will see two buttons: "OPEN" and "UNINSTALL". Touching "OPEN" will open the app on your Nexus-7. The "UNINSTALL" button will remove the app from your Nexus-7. Google gives you the opportunity to change your mind. If you decide that you don't want to buy the app within 15 minutes of purchase, your money will be refunded

4.8.2 - Uninstalling Apps from Your Nexus-7

There are two ways to remove an app entirely from your Nexus-7. The first is to revisit the Google Play Store where you originally bought the app and touch the "UNINSTALL" button. See the figure above.

The second way to remove an app from your Nexus-7 can be done on the Nexus-7 itself.

Start by finding the app on your "All Apps" page - not on your Home Screen. Touch the "All Apps Button" in this figure to open your All Apps Screen.

Now, on your All Apps Screen, touch and hold on the app icon - Angry Birds in this figure. After a second or two the two icons, "Uninstall" and "App Info" will appear at the top of the screen. Drag the icon for the app you want to uninstall onto the "Uninstall", trashcan, icon. When you raise your finger, you will be asked to confirm that you really do want to uninstall the app. Confirm and the app will be deleted entirely from your Nexus-7

4.8.3 - Quitting Apps on Your Nexus-7

When you have finished using an app on your Nexus-7, you typically leave that app's screen by touching the "Back" button or the "Home Screen" button at the bottom of the screen. That will take you to the previous screen or to your Home Screen, but it doesn't actually quit the app. The app goes dormant but is still running in the background consuming system resources. If you're not going to be using that app for some time, you might want to actually quit it - stop it from running.

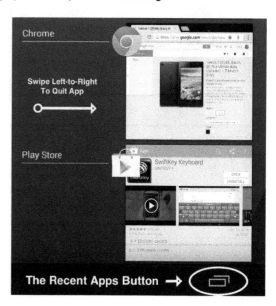

To quit an app, start by touching the "Recent" apps button at the bottom of any screen. This will open a vertical list of all the apps that are still running on your Nexus-7. The most recent app will be at the bottom of the list and the oldest app will be at the top. Find the app(s) you want to quit and swipe your finger across them in this list starting at the left side of the screen and sweeping toward the right side. This will sweep the app icon right off the screen and the space it occupied will be filled in by other apps.

4.8.4 - Essential Apps for Your Nexus-7

Your Nexus-7 comes with several apps already installed. But there are some apps that are not installed by default that you might find essential. First, let me make it clear that I am not recommending any of these apps. I am not associated with any of these app's vendors. I include them here because they are popular or because they perform actions that you might find essential to accomplish what you want to do with your Nexus-7.

When choosing an app to install on your Nexus-7 there are a few things to consider:

1) How risky is this app? Look at the permissions the app is asking for and ask yourself whether they sound reasonable. Does the free game you are considering want to be able to read your emails? If you are not comfortable granting the permissions requested, you might want to look for another app that does what you want.

2) How many people have already downloaded this app? How many have given it good reviews? You may not want to be the Guinea pig who is the first to download a malicious app.

3) Is this "free" app really worth it? Free apps often come with a lot of advertising. You might prefer to buy the paid version for a few dollars and avoid the advertising. Also consider that a paid app developer is more likely to be around to fix problems and to update the app.

There is debate as to whether or not your Nexus-7 needs anti-malware installed. I tend toward the cautious side and have installed an anti-malware app on my Nexus-7. 360 Security is one of many. It gets good reviews and is very successful in detecting malware used to test it.

"Avast" is another highly rated anti-malware app. I chose it mainly because I like the way it looks. If you decide to install an anti-malware app, make it the first app you install. That way it will be running when you install other apps and can scan them for bad things.

DO NOT INSTALL THIS APP ON YOUR NEXUS-7

This app should be installed on your mobile phone. If you install in on your Nexus-7, that will entirely defeat the purpose of 2-Step Verification since anyone with your Nexus-7 can get an authorization code.

This app gives you access to all of the files on your Nexus-7. I'm not sure that's a good idea. But if you need a file manager for some reason, this one gets very good reviews.

You can store just about anything - notes, photos, website links, and so on - in EverNote and whatever it is will be synced between all of your computers and devices that have EverNote installed.

Feedly is just one of many rss feed readers. They all do essentially the same thing. Choose one that has a user interface that you like.

If you read Kindle Books, you will want to install the Kindle Reader on your Nexus-7. There is also a Nook eBook reader available. And of course there is always Google Books

LastPass is a very well reviewed password manager. It runs on every computer and device known to man so you will have access to your passwords on every device you own. The developers seem committed to security which is good in a password manager.

If you want to be able to import photos from your camera's SD Card, you will need to install Nexus Media Importer. I will explain how to use it in a later section on Photos.

SwiftKey replaces the default Nexus keyboard. It is customizable. I like the sounds better than the ones from Google. Perhaps its best feature is that it has cursor keys to move the insertion point back and forth. A lot of people like it - you might be one of them.

There are dozens of weather apps. Choose one that looks good to you. I like this one because it has radar maps to show rain and snow.

Before leaving this section, I should mention that you can also buy Nexus-7 apps from Amazon. Amazon offers one free app per day that is normally not free. To get started with the Amazon App Store, go to this site: http://www.amazon.com/gp/mas/get/android .

4.9 - Menus and Settings

There are dozens, perhaps hundreds, of settings that I have not discussed. There are settings for individual apps. There are settings for your Nexus-7 device itself. There are settings for your Google Account, for your Gmail Account, for your Google Wallet Account, and on and on. There are several ways that you can access these settings.

We have already used the first technique several times in our discussions. Swipe downward starting anywhere above the right half of the screen This will reveal a "Quick Settings" panel where you can adjust several settings, such as screen brightness. To reveal the whole set of Nexus-7 device settings, touch the "Settings" item as illustrated in this figure.

There is a "Settings" app installed on your Nexus-7. The icon for this app looks like this illustration. Touching this icon will open the full list of Nexus-7 device settings just as using the "Quick Settings" technique described above does.

There is also a "Google Settings" app installed on your Nexus-7. The icon looks like this illustration. Touching this app will open some settings associated with your Google Account and Nexus-7 device.

You can access all of the settings for your Google Account by going to:

https://www.google.com/settings .

To access settings for individual apps, look for this "3-squares" icon. This is the Nexus-7 symbol for a menu. Touching this icon will open a menu associated with the app that you are using at the moment.

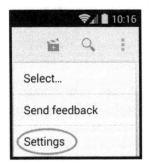

This "3-squares" menu icon is generally located in the upper right corner of the app screen as illustrated here. Touching this icon drops down a menu which, in general, contains a "Settings" item. Touching this icon will open a menu of settings for this specific app.

Some apps do not follow the "upper-right corner" convention. Some, like the Google Clock app illustrated here, put their "menu" icon somewhere else such as in the lower-right corner as is the case here. Touching this menu icon will open a pop-up menu which will, in general, contain a "Settings" item for that app.

In your spare time, you might take a look at the settings available for all of the apps you use. You may discover that you can change something that has been really bugging you about how that app works. Or, you might find that the default setting you have been using are not at all what you want.

4.10 - Notifications and Quick Settings

In the top-left corner of every Nexus-7 screen is a "mini-notifications" area.as illustrated in this figure. This area shows small icons representing the various types of Notifications you might receive. Some examples of possible Notifications are:

❖ When a new Gmail message arrives,
❖ When a Calendar reminder is due,
❖ If you upload or download files you will be notified of the progress and when the task is complete
❖ The current temperature at your location
❖ When you take a photo or screenshot
❖ And many more

In the top-right corner of every Nexus-7 screen is a "Quick Settings" area. The small icons in this area include:

❖ The current time
❖ The battery charge level
❖ Mobile data signal strength
❖ WiFi network signal strength

You can reveal a more complete listing of Notifications and Quick Settings by swiping downward starting just above the screen in the left or right halves of the screen respectively.

4.10.1 - Your Nexus-7 Notifications

If you swipe downward from the upper left half of any Nexus-7 screen, you will reveal a list of recent Notifications as illustrated here:

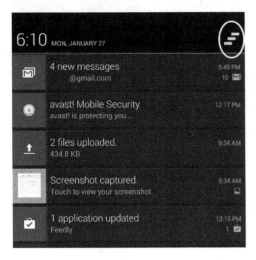

These notifications provide information. For example, in the figure at the left, the 1st and 2nd items simply tell me that 4 new email messages have arrived and that the Avast! Mobile Security app is running. But, touching any of these Notifications will open a screen with more information or that will allow me to perform some actions related to the Notification. For example, if I were to touch the 1st item, "4 new messages", that would open my Gmail app and allow me to read those messages. If I were to touch the 2nd item, "avast! Mobile Security", that would open the Avast! app and allow me to set various options for the app.

You can dismiss these Notifications, one by one, by swiping them right or left off the screen. You can dismiss all of them al once by touching the icon in the upper-right corner, shown outlined, that looks like three horizontal bars in echelon.

4.10.2 - Your Nexus-7 "Quick Settings"

If you swipe downward from the upper right half of any Nexus-7 screen, you will reveal an array of icons representing some useful settings as illustrated here:

These "Quick Settings" are a subset of all the setting for your Nexus-7. These are the ones Google has decided you are the most likely to want to set from time to time. So, for example, the 2nd icon in the upper row labeled "Brightness" allows you to adjust the screen brightness. Just touch this icon and a slider will appear. You can touch&drag this slider right and left to increase or decrease brightness. Touching each icon will open a screen that pertains to that setting. For example, touching the battery symbol that indicates 98% charge in this figure will open a screen listing all of the apps that are running and how much battery power they are consuming. You might want to experiment by touching each icon and see what they do.

The icon in the upper right corner labeled "Settings" will open a screen with all of the available settings for your Nexus-7. And, touching the icon in the upper-left corner with your account photo will sign you out of your Nexus-7 account.

5 - Setting Up Google Wallet

Google Wallet is like having a credit and/or debit card, a bank account, PayPal, many of your "loyalty cards" and a bunch of discount coupons stored in your Nexus-7. You can make purchases at thousands of stores without giving the store your credit or debit card number - think Target. You can pay for stuff online with 1 or 2 clicks and without sending your credit card number. It is pretty slick.

In the previous section we discussed how to buy apps and other stuff from the Google Play Store using Google Wallet. Since you will probably be buying a lot of stuff, apps, music, movies, books, from Google Play, having a Google Wallet will be a great time saver. And it will be more secure because you don't have to send your credit card information for every purchase.

Setting up Google Wallet is a two part process. First you have to create your Google Wallet Account and link it to your Google Account. The second step is installing and setting up the Google Wallet app on your Nexus-7.

5.1 - Setting Up Your Google Wallet Account

Setting up your Google Wallet Account is really simple. Since you already have a Google Account, all you have to do is link a Wallet Account to your Google Account.

Start by going to: https://wallet.google.com . You will be asked to provide your Google Account name and password again.

That will take you to a page like this where you provide your name and ZIP Code. If you check the "Credit or Debit Card" checkbox, you can provide credit or debit card information at this time. All the major credit cards are accepted.

You can also link your Google Wallet to a bank account and if you do that you can transfer money to and from your bank account and your Google Wallet Account. If you transfer money into your Wallet, you can use it to pay for purchases without having a credit or debit card associated with your Wallet Account. If someone sends you money, that money will appear in your Google Wallet Account cash balance.

You could stop at this point and have a useful Wallet Account that you can use from your personal computer. But to use your Wallet from your Nexus-7, you will have to install the Google Wallet app on the Nexus-7.

5.2 - Setting Up the Google Wallet App on Your Nexus-7

Start by installing the Google Wallet app on your Nexus-7. It is free from the Google Play Store

The first time you launch the Wallet app on your Nexus-7, you will see a screen like this one where you will link the Wallet Account to your main Google Account. You should see a list of all the Google Accounts you already have. Just select the account that you want to link to this Wallet.

Your Google Wallet will be protected by a four digit Personal Identification Number (PIN), just as your bank Debit Cards are. You will choose your PIN on this screen. Since this PIN will protect your money, don't choose something lame like 1234 or 5555. The idea here is to choose a PIN that will take a thief some time to guess by trial and error. Long enough for you to sign-in to your Google Account and revoke this PIN. Google also protects your Wallet by locking it after a few failed attempts to enter the correct PIN.

You can also set a timeout after which your Wallet will lock itself. You get to this screen by touching the Wallet app menu icon (remember those 3 stacked squares from Section 4.9) and opening the Wallet "Settings" item. Part way down these settings will be the "Wallet PIN" setting as illustrated here. Touch the "PIN Timeout" setting. Your choices are to lock your Wallet after 15 minutes, after 24 hours, or never. Obviously the "Never" choice is the same as not having a PIN.

NOTE: Once your Google Wallet is locked, you will need to have Internet access to unlock it again.

OK, you have installed the Google Wallet app on your Nexus-7, you have selected a PIN to protect that Wallet, and you have set a timeout after which the Wallet will lock itself. So, now, what can you do with this Google Wallet?

5.3 - Making Financial Transactions with Your Google Wallet

It turns out that you can do a lot of things with your Google Wallet:

5.3.1 - Buying Stuff from the Google Play Store

Buying stuff from Google Play will probably be your most frequent use of Google Wallet. Once you have linked a Wallet Account to your Google Account, you will see the Google Wallet icon next to the "Buy" buttons in the Google Play Store. Just touch the "Buy" button and the purchase will be charged to your Google Wallet Account.

5.3.2 - Buying Stuff from Online Vendors

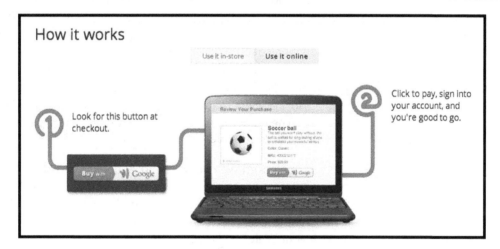

When you're shopping online look for the "Buy with Google" logo at checkout. If you see it, you can touch it and your purchase will be charged to your Google Wallet Account. No need to send your credit card information since Google already has it.

The number of online merchants is growing daily so you just have to look for the Google logo at checkout when you shop online. Here are some online stores that take Google payments right now:

5.3.3 - Buying Stuff from Brick and Mortar Stores

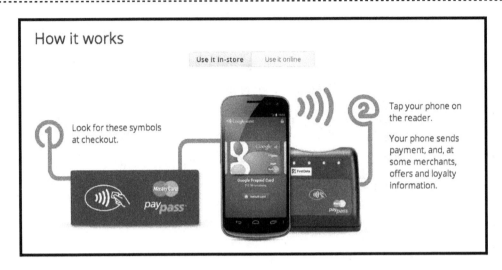

You can use your Nexus-7 to pay with your Google Wallet Account at any store that accepts Master Card "PayPass". Look for these logos at the checkout card reader (step 1 in this figure). Stores that accept Google Wallet payments at checkout have special card readers that not only read credit and debit cards but also have "Near Field Communication" (NFC) built into the card reader. Your Nexus-7 also has NFC capability. So, you can pay by simply holding your Nexus-7 close to the card reader. By close, I mean really, really close. The range of NFC is only a couple of inches at best so you basically have to touch the back of your Nexus-7 to the card reader in order for the NFC connection to be made. Your Nexus-7 has to be "awake", i.e. The screen has to be on, in order to pay this way. Be sure to always select "Credit" if prompted on the credit card machine in the store.

Your Google Wallet Account must also be unlocked with your PIN to enable payment by NFC. The downside of this is that you have to have Internet access in order to unlock with your PIN. If you have a Nexus-7 with mobile data capability (LTE), this shouldn't be a problem. But if your Nexus-7 doesn't have mobile data capability, if you will want to use your Nexus-7 to make payments at stores, you should probably enter your PIN to unlock your Wallet while you are still at home. You will also have to set the PIN Timeout Period to be "24-hours" so that your Wallet doesn't re-lock itself during your shopping (see Section 5.2).

Finding Stores that Accept Google Wallet Payments:

As I mentioned, stores that accept MasterCard "PayPass" also accept Google Wallet payments. MasterCard has a website where you can find stores in your area that accept payment by Google Wallet: http://www.mastercard.us/cardholder-services/paypass-locator.html

There is also an app for that. You can install the MasterCard PayPass Locator app on your Nexus-7 and find stores near your current location that will take your Google Wallet for payment.

Here are some popular merchants that currently (early 2014) accept payment using Google Wallet. I also used the store finder website mentioned above and found several stores within a few miles of my house: Rite-Aid, McDonalds, Chevron, CVS, Jack in the Box, PetCo, and Home Depot.

5.3.4 - Sending Money to People

You can send money to anyone with an email address, but they will not be able to receive that money unless they have a Google Wallet Account. There are two ways to send money:

Send Money from the Google Wallet App

Launch your Google Wallet app. You will be asked to enter your PIN to unlock your Wallet. This will take you to a screen similar to the one illustrated at the left where you can enter an email address, or the name of someone from your Contacts that you want to send money to.

That will take you to this screen where you enter the amount you want to send. If your Google Wallet Account has a sufficient cash balance, that will be used. If you don't have cash in your account, then your linked credit or debit card will be used. If you use a credit card, there will be an additional fee of 2.9% or $0.30 whichever is larger. You can also add a message to your "gift". When you are done entering the

information, touch the "Send" icon shown outlined in the upper-right corner of the previous figure. It looks like a paper airplane.

The recipient of your money will receive an email message like this. If they have a Google Wallet Account, all they have to do is click on the "Claim $..." button and the money will be transferred from your Account to theirs. If they don't have a Google Wallet Account, they will be encouraged to open one. If they do not claim the money within 14 days, it will be returned, minus the fee, to your Account.

In order to send money, you will have to prove that you are who you say you are by providing information known by "third party" companies such as credit reporting agencies. This could be stuff such as the street number you lived at 25 years ago, or the name of the city you lived in in 1987, or something similar.

Both sender and receiver of "Google" money must live in the US, must be 18 years or older, and must have a Google Wallet Account.

Send Money from Gmail

You can now attach money to a Gmail message. Just click on the "$" symbol in the row of attachable items at the bottom of your Gmail message shown outlined in this figure. From that point, the process is the same as described above.

5.3.5 - Google "Offers"

Sometimes, merchants that accept Google Wallet payments will make special "offers" available to Google users such as yourself. You receive and manage these offers via an app that you can install free from the Google Play Store.

The first time you run the Google Offers app, it will tell you a little about how Offers work. It will also present you with this window where it gives you the opportunity to turn "Nearby Notifications" ON or OFF. The idea is that as you travel around, if

Google Offers finds an offer nearby, it will send you a Notification so that you might take advantage of that offer. If you live in a small town where there are not many offers, you might like to turn these "Nearby Notifications" ON. But, if you live in New York, you may be inundated with constant Offers Notifications. In that case you might want to turn "Nearby Notifications" OFF.

For example, here's an offer from a brew-pub near where I live. It is offering 25% off the cost of any item during some days and times. If I think I might want to take advantage of this offer, I would touch the "Get Offer" button shown outlined in the figure. When I do that the offer gets saved in "My Offers" folder. I can redeem the offer later by going to "My Offers".

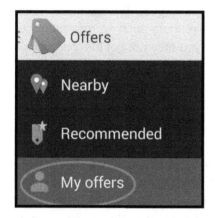

To go to your saved "My Offers" just touch the Offers app icon shown in the upper-left corner of this figure. That will drop down the menu you see in the figure. Touch the "My Offers" item shown outlined. That will open a listing of your Saved Offers. The figure below shows only the first in my list of offers - the one I saved above.

To redeem the offer when I go to the store offering it, I just touch inside the offer shown in the illustration to the right. That will open a window, part of which is illustrated below.

This window tells me how to redeem the offer. In this case I just have to show it to the vendor. In some cases there may be a bar code that the vendor has to scan.

This window has a lot more information that I have not shown here. There is a map showing where the store making the offer is located and any other details I might need to know about the offer. Touch "Redeem Offer" when you do that.

There are several settings for the Google Offers app. This figure shows a portion of the Settings having to do with Notifications. As I mentioned above, Notifications could become annoying if there are too many of them. These Settings allow you to customize when you get notified. For example, you might want to be notified when one of your saved offers is about to expire or when there is a new offer nearby. Check the boxes you like and un-check those you don't want.

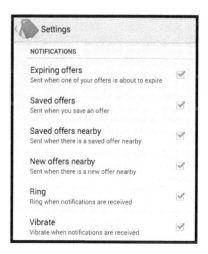

5.3.6 - Things to Note About Google Wallet

Google Wallet and "Reward" Cards

When you make a payment using your Google Wallet, that payment shows up on your credit card as going to Google, not to the actual vendor you paid. That means that if your linked credit card is a "cash-back" or other reward card, you may not get the "reward" you expect. For example, some reward cards give bigger rewards for purchases at certain kinds of vendors such as restaurants or gas stations. If you use your Google Wallet at one of these vendors, you may not get the the "bigger" reward you expect.

Google Purchase Protection

"Google Wallet Purchase Protection" offers protection against fraudulent use of your Google Wallet Account. It covers 100% of all "eligible" unauthorized transactions if you report them within 180 days from the day the fraudulent transaction was made. A lot of stuff is not "eligible" for protection. Purchases from "Google Properties" such as Google Play and YouTube are not covered. Any transaction that was made in error, you sent the money to the wrong email address for example, is not covered. I think the best part of "Google Wallet Purchase Protection" is that Google monitors all transactions made using your Google Wallet and tries to identify fraudulent use.

Google Wallet Pre-Paid Debit Card

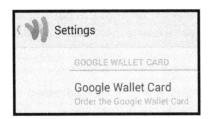

You can get a real, physical Debit Card associated with your Google Wallet Account. This card will give you access to the cash balance in your Account and it works just like any other debit card. You can use this card to make payments or to make cash withdrawals at ATM machines. ATM machine fees may apply. To request a Google Wallet Card, go to the Google Wallet app's Settings and touch the "Order the Google Wallet Card" button shown in this figure.

6 - Setting Up Google Cloud Print

In the "old days" you connected a printer to your personal computer and installed drivers for that printer on your computer. This approach doesn't work with the Nexus-7. One of the things that makes it possible to build a Nexus-7 with only 16 GB of memory is that it doesn't contain print drivers for the thousands of printers currently in use. In fact, the Nexus-7 has only a single print driver - one for "Google Cloud Print". But, before you can print using Google Cloud Print, you have to set it up.

There are three ways to print documents from your Nexus-7:

1) Print to a Shared Printer connected to your personal computer   (Section 6.1)

2) Print to a Cloud Print Enabled printer   (Section 6.2)

3) Print to a PDF file and then print that PDF file from your personal computer   (Section 6.3)

Each of these approaches is described in the following sections.

6.1 - Printing to Printers Shared by Your Personal Computer

You can "share" the printers already attached to your personal computer - Mac or Windows - so that you can print to them from your Nexus-7. To do this your computer must be connected to the internet and you must have the Chrome Browser installed on your personal computer and that browser must be signed-in to the same Google Account as the Nexus-7 you are printing from.

6.1.1 - Connecting Shared Printers to Google Cloud Print

So, the **first step** in setting up a shared printer for your Nexus-7 is to download and install the Chrome Browser on your Mac or Windows computer if you have not already done that. You can download the Chrome web browser free from the Google site

https://www.google.com/intl/en/chrome/browser/

The **second step** in setting up a shared printer for your Nexus-7 is to enable sharing of the printer(s) attached to your personal computer. For example, on a Mac:

1) Go to "System Preferences" and open the "Sharing" preference pane.
2) Click on "Printer Sharing" and then click on the checkboxes next to the printers you want to share.

On a Windows 7 PC it's a little more complicated:

1) Click "Start"
2) Click "Control Panel"
3) In the Search Box, type "Network"

4)   Click "Network and Sharing Center"

5)   In the left pane, click "Change Advanced Sharing Settings"

6)   Click the down pointing chevron to expand the network profile

7)   Turn on File and Printer Sharing if it isn't already on

8)   Click "Save"

9)   Now, Click "Start" again

10) Click "Devices and Printers"

11) Right-click the printer you want to share and select "Printer Properties"

12) Click the "Sharing" tab

13) Check the "Share this Printer" checkbox

The **third step** is to add the shared printers to the "Google Cloud Print Connector" that is built into the Chrome Browser on your personal computer - Mac or Windows.

1)   Sign-in to the user account on your personal computer that contains the Chrome Browser that is signed into the Google Account that you want to print from on your Nexus-7.

2)   Launch the Chrome Browser

3)   Click the "3-horizontal bar" icon near the upper right of the window and select "Settings"

4)   Click "Show Advanced Settings" near the bottom of the Settings window

5)   Scroll down to "Google Cloud Print"

6)   Click "Add Printers". If no printers are connected to this Google Account this link is titled "Add Printers". If a printer is connected, this link is titled "Open Google Cloud Print".

7)   If prompted, Sign-In to the same Google Account that you will be printing from on your Nexus-7. If you have set up 2-Step Verification you may have to use one of your Application Specific Passwords instead of your regular account password at this point.

8)   Click on the blue button "Add Printers". This adds all the printers shared by this personal computer to Google Cloud Print for this Google Account.

6.1.2 - Printing to Shared Printers from Your Nexus-7

Printing from Android devices is a work in progress. Google is constantly upgrading and changing its printing capabilities. At this time, you can print using the Google "Cloud Print" plugin that comes pre-installed on your Nexus-7. Or, there are third-party apps that you can use to print from your Nexus-7. Some of these apps have more features than Google "Cloud Print" does at this time. I will discuss printing using Google "Cloud Print" first and then printing using third party apps in the next section.

6.1.3 - Printing Using Google "Cloud Print"

Your Nexus-7 comes with "Cloud Print" from Google installed. This plugin will allow you to print some things to any printer connected to Google Cloud Print on your personal computer. I'll use a PDF file stored in my Google Drive as an example of printing using Google "Cloud Print".

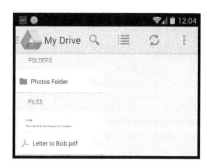

As an example of printing PDF files I have opened the Google Drive app on my Nexus-7. I will discuss Google Drive in a later section. For right now, this figure illustrates that I have a "Photos Folder" and a PDF file named "Letter to Bob" in my Google Drive. Touching the "Letter to Bob" item opens the file as illustrated in the following figure.

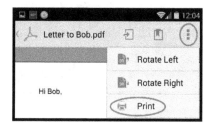

Touching the "Menu" icon outlined in the upper-right corner of this figure opens a drop-down menu as shown. One of the items in this menu is "Print". Touching "Print" opens the Print Dialog illustrated below-right.

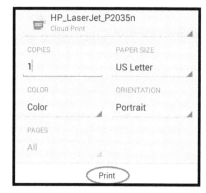

The Print Dialog shows that this file will be printed to the HP_LaserJet_P2035n that is connected to my Mac and that I have shared with Google Cloud Print as explained in the previous section. If you have more than one printer attached to Google Cloud Print, you can choose which of them to use to print this file by touching the small triangle in the lower-right corner of the printer name field. You can also adjust other printer settings by touching the other fields. When you have things set up as you like, touching "Print", shown outlined, will send your job to the selected printer.

You can print photos using Google "Cloud Print". The Nexus-7 has two different, but almost identical photo apps installed. One is "Gallery" and the other is "Photos". The reason for this duplication of apps is lost in the mists of time and I'm sure that Google will eventually eliminate one of them. For right now, printing photos from these two apps is slightly different.

Printing Photos from "Photos":

Touching the "Photos" app icon will launch your "Photos" app and display the photos you have stored with it as illustrated to the right. Touch the photo you want to print and that will open that photo as shown to the left. Touch the menu icon in the upper-right corner and then touch the "Print" item. That will open a Print Dialog as illustrated above where you can choose which printer to send the print job to and other items.

Printing Photos from "Gallery":

Printing photos from "Gallery" is similar to printing them from "Photos". You launch the "Gallery" app by touching its icon. Then you find the photo you want to print in your Gallery "Albums". Touch the photo you want. Then touch the menu icon in the upper-right corner of the window. That will drop down a menu as illustrated to the right. The last item in this menu will be "Print". Touching that will open the Print Dialog where you can choose which printer to use and other printing settings.

The menu in Gallery is different from that in Photos, but the result is the same.

Printing Other Types of Files.

Google Cloud Print can print a web page from the Chrome Browser as illustrated at the left. Just touch the menu icon and then "Print" as we have done in the last two illustrations. It cannot print Gmail messages directly, but you can open the Chrome Browser and navigate to your Gmail Account, open a Gmail message and then print that webpage.

And, you can print documents you have created with the "Quick Office" app from Google. The figure at the right illustrates printing a "Word" document created using Quick Office.

At this time (January 2014) you cannot print Google Docs, nor Calendars nor Google Keep Notes, nor Persons contact information. By the time you read this, those capabilities may have been added to Google Cloud Print. Until then, you can use third party apps that have expanded printing capabilities.

Printing Using Third Party Apps

Two third party printing apps that have received good reviews are "Cloud Print" by Paulo Fernendes. Although this app has the same name, this is **not** Google's "Cloud Print". You can install the app free from the Google Play Store and test its features, but the free version has ads. To eliminate the ads, you will need to make an in-app purchase of an unlock key that costs $2.60.

Another printing app that has received good reviews is "Printer Share" by Dynamax. Once again the trial version is free, but the full version costs $13 from the Google Play Store.

I cannot recommend either of these apps since I have not tried them. It all depends upon whether Google Cloud Print can currently print the types of documents you want to print. If you need to print Calendars or Persons contact information, then one of these third party apps may be just what you need.

6.2 - Printing to "Cloud Print Enabled" Printers

Cloud Print Enabled printers are relatively new. "Cloud Print Enabled" is the Chrome name for this class of printers. Other vendors have different names. Apple calls them "Air Print Enabled", HP calls them "ePrint Enabled", and so forth. These printers all work the same way and all of them will work with your Nexus-7.

Cloud Print Enabled printers are not connected to your computer, but rather to the Internet - possibly through your local area network (LAN). A personal computer is not needed for Cloud Print enabled printers. All of the data and instructions for printing are delivered to the printer via the Internet from a website maintained by the printer's manufacturer. Basically, you send the document you want printed to the manufacturer's website and that website then sends printing instructions directly to your printer. You send the document you want to print as an email attachment to the email address assigned to your printer as will be described below.

The following description of how to set up a Google Cloud Print Enabled printer is based on the HP 401n printer. I suspect that setting up other printers from other vendors will work in a similar way. There will be specific instructions for setting up your printer included with the printer.

6.2.1 - Setting Up a Cloud Print Enabled Printer

Setting up a Cloud Print Enabled printer is a three step process described in these sections:

6.2.1.1) Connect your Cloud Print Enabled printer to the manufacturer's website and obtain an unique email address for your printer.

6.2.1.2) Connect your printer to Google Chrome using the Google Cloud Print Connector

6.2.1.3) Connect your printer to your iPhone, iPad or Android devices.

6.2.1.1 - Obtain an Unique eMail Address for Your Cloud Print Enabled Printer

Step 1) Set up your printer according to the manufacturer's instructions. This will include connecting the printer to your LAN via an Ethernet cable or a WiFi network connection.

Important Note: If you connect your printer to your personal computer using a USB or other cable, it cannot be used as a Cloud Print Enabled printer. You must connect your Cloud Print Enabled printer directly to a network that has Internet access, not to a computer.

Near the end of the setup process, the printer will print out a page of information. This information contains two important items:

1) The IP address assigned to the printer by your router. For example, my HP 401's LAN address is 10.0.1.193. You will need this IP address to connect with the printer's built in website.

2) A "Claim Code" that identifies your printer to the manufacturer in order to obtain an email address for that specific printer.

You might want to keep this information for future reference.

Step 2) Using any LAN connected computer enter the printer's IP address in the Omnibar of the Chrome Browser. So, for example, I entered 10.0.1.193 in the Omnibar of my Chrome browser. This will connect you to a web page that is built into your printer. This web page will allow you to make various settings and to check on things like toner or ink supply levels.

With the HP 401n printer, this built in web page also allows me to connect to the "HP Web Services" website. The first thing I had to do on this site was to accept the "Terms of Use" to enable HP Web Services. This took me to the "HP ePrint Center". You will, of course, go to the website for your particular brand of printer - not necessarily to the HP site.

Step 3) Create an "HP Connected Account". This involves entering a valid email address and creating a password. You must also agree to the "HP Connected Terms of Use".

Step 4) Add your device to your HP Connected Account. This will require the "Claim Code" that the printer printed at the end of Step 1. I gave HP my Claim Code and HP gave me an unique email address for my printer. My printer's email address looks like **********@hpeprint.com . You will have the opportunity to change this address if you choose to. You definitely want to save this address. You will need it every time you print something. I entered this address into my Contacts list using the name "HP Printer". So, whenever I want to print something, I can just email it to "HP Printer".

Step 5) Limit ePrint access to your printer. Right now, anyone that has your printer's email address can send stuff and your printer will print it. This could turn into the print version of spam. To prevent this from happening, you can limit access to your printer to just a few "From" email addresses. Remember that to print a document you attach it to an email message and send that message to your printer's email address. The email address from which you send the message is the "From" address. So, if you send your email messages from your Gmail account, it is that Gmail account address that you will use to limit access to your printer. HP Connect allows you to enter a list of email addresses that are allowed to print to your printer. You will probably enter all the email addresses that you and any family members or fellow workers use so that they can all print to your printer. HP will send a confirmation message to all of the email addresses you list.

That's it. Your Cloud Print Enabled printer is now all set up. You can test it by composing a brief email message and sending it to your printer's email address. After a brief wait, the message should be printed. If this doesn't work, you will have to refer to your printer vendor's support site for help.

Important Note: If you enter any text in the body of an email message, that is what will get printed. Any attachment will be ignored. So, if you want to print a document, attach it to a blank email message.

6.2.2 - Connect Your Printer Using the Google Cloud Print Connector
----

At this point you can print to your Cloud Print Enabled printer by attaching the document to be printed to an email message and then sending that message to your printer's email address. That works, but it becomes cumbersome if you want to print several documents. Fortunately, there is an easier way. If you connect your printer to your Google Cloud Print Account, then that printer will appear in the list of possible printers when you select "Print" when using any application.

Google Cloud Print is still a work in progress, so what you see on your screen may be slightly different from what is shown in the following figures.

To connect your Cloud Print Enabled printer, you will have to visit the Chrome Cloud Print Settings page:

- Launch the Chrome Browser

- Click the "3-horizontal bar" icon near the upper right of the window and select "Settings"

- Near the bottom of the Settings window click "Show Advanced Settings"

- Scroll down to "Google Cloud Print" and click on "Manage Print Settings ..." as shown here. If you have never connected a printer before, this button will be labeled "Open Cloud Print".

This will open a page, part of which is illustrated in the figure to the right. Just click on "Add a Cloud Ready Printer" and that will take you to another page, part of which is illustrated in the figure below.

In the figure illustrated at the left, first select the manufacturer of your Cloud Ready Printer. This will display a screen specific to your type of printer. The page illustrated in this figure is specific to HP printers, so what you see may be quite different. The "Setup Instructions" shown in this figure end with the admonition to click on the "HP Registration Page" link. Do that and it will take you to a site specific to your printer. The one illustrated on the next page is specific to HP printers.

Simply fill in the email address assigned to your printer and click on "Connect My Printer". That's all there is to it. If everything has worked out as expected, you will now see your Cloud Ready printer listed as one of the destinations for any document you print as is illustrated in the figure below. The HP_Laserjet_P2035 is the printer connected to my Mac and shared with Google Cloud Print and the HP_LasrJet_400_M401n is the Cloud Print Enabled printer I have just connected to Google Cloud Print.

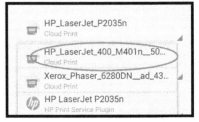

At this point, you no longer have to send documents as email attachments in order to have them printed. Just call up the print dialog in any app that supports printing and select your Cloud Enabled printer from the list of possible destinations as is illustrated in the figure above.

Important Note: Remember that when you print a document to a Cloud Enabled printer from any vendor and from any device, that document gets transmitted to the printer vendor's servers where it is stored briefly during the printing process. All of the printer vendors say that they will delete your document as soon as the print job has finished, but who knows? Don't print anything that you consider "sensitive" using any Cloud Enabled printer. Better to "print" it to a PDF file and then transfer that to your personal computer using Google Drive. You can then print that file to a printer connected to your personal computer. I will explain this process in the next section.

6.3 - Printing to a PDF File in Your Google Drive

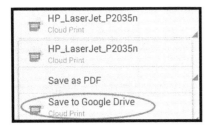

When you print a document, a "Print Dialog" will open with a list of available printers as illustrated in the figure to the left. "Save to Google Drive" will be one of these printers. If you choose "Save to Google Drive" as your print destination, the page will be converted to a PDF file and that file will be put in your Google Drive. You can then sign into the Google Account from which you sent the print job and you should find the PDF file in the Google Drive on your personal computer. I have found that Google Drive doesn't always sync right away. To force a sync, find the Google Drive app on your personal computer and launch it. Nothing apparent happens, but now you will find your PDF file in the Google Drive folder on your personal computer. You can now drag the PDF file out of Google Drive and save it anywhere you choose on your personal computer. This file can be opened and printed by whatever app handles PDF files on your personal computer: "Preview" on the Mac and "Adobe Acrobat Reader" on Windows machines. This option is particularly useful if you have a printer attached to your personal computer but it isn't "connected" to your Google Account.

7 - Setting Up Google Drive

7.1 - What is Google Drive?

There are two places on your Nexus-7 that your documents, photos and other files can be stored. One is on your Nexus-7 itself using the 16 or 32 GB of internal storage built into the Nexus-7. The other place is Google Drive. Google Drive appears to be an app on your Nexus-7, but in reality it is a block of storage space on Google's servers that is assigned to your Google Account.

It is important to understand the distinction between these two types of storage:

- The on-your-device files can be accessed without an internet connection because they are actually stored on your device.

- Files stored in your Google Drive can only be accessed when you have an internet connection. So, if you want to work on a file when you are offline, you must "download" it from Google Drive to your Nexus-7 while you have an internet connection.

When you "download" a file, you are transferring it from Google Drive to your Nexus-7 device's internal storage. When you "upload" a file, you are transferring it from your Nexus-7 device up to the Google Drive cloud servers.

You can access your Google Drive from any computer with internet access. Any files you put in Google Drive can be accessed from any computer with internet access. Any changes you make to the contents of your Google Drive are automatically synced to the Google servers and thence to any computers or other Android devices with access to your Drive. This is by far the easiest and most secure way to transfer files between your Nexus-7 and your personal computer.

There are three ways to access your Google Drive:

1) Using your Nexus-7   (section 7.2)
2) Using Your Personal Computer (section 7.3)
3) Using a Web Browser   (section 7.4)

You may ask why I'm going to describe items 2 and 3. After all, isn't this a book about the Nexus-7? Yes it is, but as I said a short while ago, using Google Drive is the easiest way to transfer files between your Nexus-7 and your other internet connected devices such as your personal computer so you have to know how to operate Google Drive on these other devices as well.

7.2 - Google Drive on Your Nexus-7

 Google Drive appears to be an app on your Nexus-7. Its icon appears on your Home Screen along with the icons for other apps. You can buy this "app" from the Goggle Play Store just like any other app. And indeed Google Drive does have applications hidden within it. But fundamentally, Google Drive is a block of storage on Google Servers somewhere in the "cloud". The apps "hidden" in Google Drive enable you to

create documents directly in Google Drive from your Nexus-7. At this time, you can only create word processing documents and spreadsheet documents. But Google has many more apps that work in Google Drive on the Chrome OS so it is only a matter of time until there will be more apps that can create documents in Google Drive on Android devices like your Nexus-7.

If you have not used Google Drive before, the Google Drive on your Nexus-7, will be empty as illustrated in this figure. You can put stuff into your Google Drive using your Nexus-7 in various ways. The reason I say "various" is because Google Drive is still a work in progress and its use is a little fragmented at this time. The best way to put an item into Google Drive depends upon what that item is. So I will discuss several different ways to store your files on Google Drive.

7.2.1 - Creating Documents in Your Google Drive

As I mentioned above, when you create a document file on your Nexus-7, that file is stored automatically in your Google Drive. It is not stored on your Nexus-7 itself, but rather up in the cloud somewhere on Google Servers. That makes it easy to access that file from any computer anywhere in the world. It also makes it easy to share that document with other people you know.

To get started, launch the Google Drive "app". At the bottom of the Google Drive window there is a row of icons as illustrated at the left. To Create a new document, touch the "Create" icon shown outlined. That will open a window as illustrated at the right where you can choose what it is that you want to create. You can create a new Folder in your Google Drive to help organize the files you put there. But for now, you can create a new word processing document which Google calls simply a "Document". Or you can create a new spreadsheet document. As I mentioned, there will be other types of documents that you will be able to create as time goes by.

These word processing and spreadsheet documents are actually created by an app called "Quick Office" that is owned by Google. Google is building the functionality of Quick Office into Google Drive. You can also "buy" (it's free) Quick Office from the Google Play Store and run it as a separate app. Using Quick Office directly, you can create PowerPoint-like slide presentations as well as word processing and spreadsheet documents. Documents created using Quick Office are stored in your Google Drive just as if you had created them in the Google Drive app itself.

For this illustration, I touched the "Document" icon in the "Create" menu. This created a new word document as illustrated in the top figure on the next page.

This figure illustrates a word document created in my Google Drive. I have named the document file "My First Doc" and entered some text. The really great thing about Google's approach to all this is shown just below the name of the document. It says "All changes saved". Every few seconds, the document being created is saved to the Google Drive servers. If

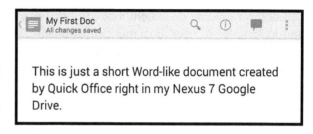

your Nexus-7 were to fail while you were typing the document, you would lose nothing except perhaps the last few characters you had typed. You could go to any other computer in the world and sign-in to your Google Account and continue typing your document just as if nothing had happened.

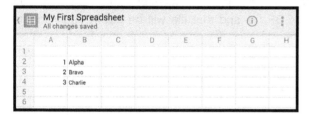

Continuing with this example, I have also created a new Spreadsheet document. It is illustrated at the left. Note again those magic words "All changes saved".

After creating those two document files, my Google Drive looks like this. The two files are safely stored on the Google Drive servers somewhere.

Files stored in your Google Drive are only available when you have an internet connection. What about those times when you are without an internet connection?

You cannot create a new document when you are offline. You cannot edit documents stored in your Google Drive when you are offline. So, what do

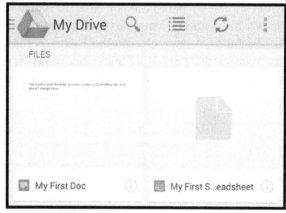

you do? Google to the rescue. Google allows Google Drive documents to be downloaded to your Nexus-7 device so that they can be edited while offline. Google calls this "Offline" access and you have to set it up while you have an internet connection.

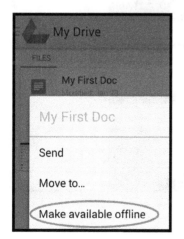

To make a document available offline, while you are online, go to your Google Drive and find the file you want. Touch-and-Hold on that document. After a few seconds, a menu will drop down, a portion of which is illustrated at the left. Touch "Make available offline". When you do that two things happen. First the document is downloaded to your Nexus-7. Second, Google installs a simplified version of Quick Office on your Nexus-7 so that you have an offline app available to edit your offline document.

Now, since you cannot create a new document while offline, but you can edit an existing document that you have made available offline, there is a simple "trick" to allow you to "create" a "new" document while offline. The trick is to create one or more blank documents while you are online and then to make these blank documents available offline. Then, when you are offline, you can edit one of these blank documents in effect "creating" a new document.

7.2.2 - Printing to a PDF File in Your Google Drive

You can put anything you can "print" into your Google Drive. When you print any document, a "Print Dialog" opens with a list of available printers as illustrated to the left. "Save to Google Drive" will be one of these printers. If you choose "Save to Google Drive" as your print destination, the page will be converted to a PDF file and that file will be put in your Google Drive.

7.2.3 - Upload Photos from Your Nexus-7 to Your Google Drive

When you take a photo with the Nexus-7's built in camera, or when you take a screenshot, that image file will be stored on your Nexus-7 in two different places. As I have mentioned previously (section 6.1.2), there are two apps on the Nexus-7 that handle image files: an app named "Photos" and an app named "Gallery". They both work pretty much the same way so I will only discuss the "Photos" app which I have used extensively in the preparation of the photos in this book.

Launch the Photos app by touching its icon as illustrated at the left. That will open the app and you can navigate through the folders to find the photo you want to upload to Google Drive. On the screen illustrated at the right, you will find the easiest way to backup this and all future photos. Just "Turn ON" Auto Backup. With Auto Backup ON every photo you take will be automatically uploaded to your Google+ Account. This is not the same as uploading it to your Google Drive, but I thought I would mention it anyway.

To upload a photo from the Photos app to Google Drive, start by navigating to the photo(s) you want to move to your Google Drive and then touch the menu icon shown outlined in the figure to the right. That will drop down a menu with only a single item, "Select" as is shown in this figure. Touch "Select" and then touch to select every photo you want to upload. When you touch a photo, a checkmark will appear as illustrated on the next page. You can also ignore the "Select" menu and just touch and hold on the first photo you want to select. Eventually, a checkmark will appear. You can then simply tap on other photos to "check" them

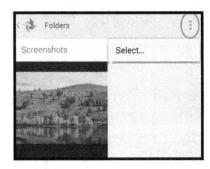

Once you have "checked" all of the photos you want to move to your Google Drive, touch the "Share" icon shown outlined in this figure. I guess this icon is supposed to represent people connected to one another.

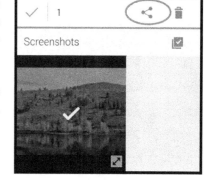

Touching the Share icon opens a window with an array of icons representing the various ways you can "share" your photo. A small portion of this array is illustrated just below.

The top row of icons labeled "People", "Circles", and "Public" represent people you are connected to via Google+. Google+ is Google's version of Facebook. If you touch "People", you can share your photos with individuals you know. "Circles" allows you to share your photos with a group of people, your "Friends" for example. And "Public" allows you to share your photos with everybody.

Also note that you can "Share" your photo via Gmail. Touch the Gmail icon and that will launch the Gmail app with your photo attached to a new message. Just fill in the destination and any message you like and touch "Send". Your photo will be sent off to your friend's email account. There are many other ways in which you can Share your photos.

But, I have drifted a little away from the topic at hand here. The icon we want to touch is the one outlined in the figure above-left, the one labelled "Drive". That will "Share" your photos with your Google Drive by uploading a copy of the photos to the Google Drive servers. You will be presented with this dialog where you confirm by touching "OK" that you do indeed want to send your photos to your Google Drive. That's all there is to it. Your photos can now be accessed from any computer in the world - after signing-in to your Google Account.

7.2.4 - Scan Documents from Your Nexus-7 to Your Google Drive

The third icon at the bottom of the Google Drive screen is "Scan" as illustrated at the right. The intent of "Scan" is to take a picture of a paper document, for example a business card, using the camera on your Nexus-7. But this photo is treated differently from "regular" photos. First, it is saved as a PDF file rather than as an image file. But the big difference is that once your scanned PDF file is uploaded to your Google Drive, Google uses powerful Optical Character Recognition (OCR) software to convert the image of any text in the PDF file into text that can be edited or searched.

For example, using my Nexus-7 I have "scanned" a business card from my wife's favorite jeweler as illustrated in the figure at the left. This is a portion of a screenshot that shows what the screen looks like when you take a "scan". Touching the blue button at the bottom of the figure takes the "scan" which is then converted into a PDF file and stored in your Google Drive.

The figure below is a portion of a screenshot taken from the screen of my Macintosh showing the contents of my Google Drive. The highlighted item is the "scanned" document and it is a PDF file. Right-clicking on this file drops down the menu where I have selected "Open With" and that drops down another menu where I have selected "Google Docs".

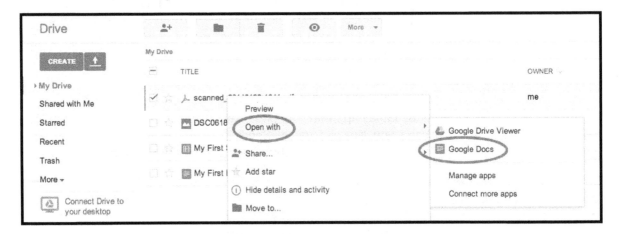

Remember that "Google Docs" is Google's name for a word processing file. So, I am asking that the PDF file, which is just a picture of the business card, should be opened in a word processing app. The figure below shows the results.

In the upper portion of this figure is the actual image of the business card and below that is the extracted text. This text is fully editable and searchable. Google OCR technology even recognizes the phone number as being a phone number and makes it into a clickable link.

To demonstrate that this is text and not just another photo of text, I have used the Google Docs "Find" function to search for the word "hours" and you can see that the search has found and highlighted that word.

You can "Scan" and convert any paper document, even a photograph that contains text, into a fully editable word processing document.

7.2.5 - Upload a File from Your Nexus-7 to Your Google Drive

When you take a screenshot that image file gets stored in your Nexus-7's built in memory. To transfer that image file, or any other file, to your Google Drive you "Upload" it. You start this process by touching the Upload icon at the bottom of the Google Drive screen.

Touching the Upload button will open a window showing a list of all the files, excluding photos, that are stored in your built-in memory. Uploading photos to your Google Drive is discussed in Section 7.2.3. In this illustration there is only one file, a screenshot, in my Nexus-7's built-in memory. Touch the file you

want to Upload and it will be instantly Uploaded to your Google Drive. The file remains stored on your Nexus-7 as well.

As an example, the following two figures show the contents of my Google Drive Before (left) and After (right) touching the Upload button followed by touching the file I wanted to Upload - a Screenshot in this example.

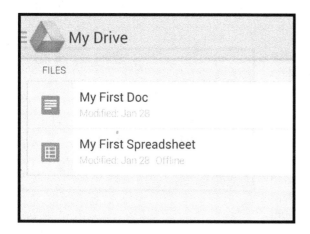
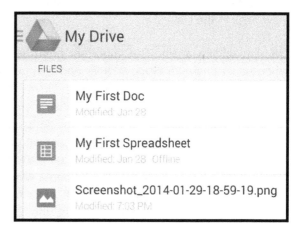

So, this is an alternate to the technique I discussed in Section 7.2.3 that is useful for uploading Screenshots.

7.2.6 - Removing Files from Your Google Drive

In the previous sections I have discussed various ways to put files into your Google Drive. In this section I will discuss how to remove them using your Nexus-7. You can also remove files from your Google Drive using any internet connected computer in the world. I will discuss this a little later.

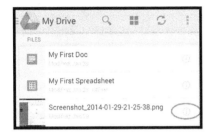 

To remove a file from your Google Drive using your Nexus-7, start by launching the Google Drive app. This will show a list of all the files currently stored in your Google Drive as illustrated in these two figures. They both show the same thing. On the left is a "List" view of my files and on the right is a "Grid" view. You can switch between these two views by touching the small icon just to the right of the search magnifying glass icon at the top of the screen. The figure at the left is a "List" view and the 2x2 array of small squares is the icon you would touch to switch to the "Grid" view. There is an icon just to the right of the search magnifying glass icon in the figure at the right, but it is cropped out of this illustration. It looks like a list and touching it will switch from the Grid view back to the List view.

OK, I'm drifting again. The important point here is that when you launch the Google Drive app and get a listing of the files currently in your Google Drive, it doesn't matter which view you use. In either view, there will be a small icon that looks like the letter "i" inside a small circle associated with each file. This icon is shown outlined in both of the figures above. Touch this icon briefly on the file you want to remove and that will open a window such as the one illustrated in this figure. There is a standard Android, three square, menu icon in the upper-right corner of this window as outlined in the figure. Touch this icon and that will reveal a menu of possible actions to take with this file.

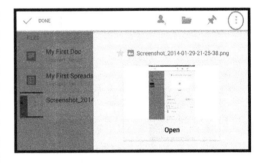

As illustrated in the figure at the right, one of these possible actions is "Remove". Touch "Remove" and you will be presented with a dialog box giving you the opportunity to confirm or cancel the removal. If you touch "OK" in this dialog, the file will be gone before you know it.

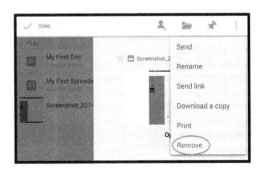

7.3 -Google Drive on Your Personal Computer

You can access your Google Drive using any internet connected computer. On a Macintosh or Windows personal computer this is accomplished most easily by installing a Google Drive "app" on your computer. You can download the Drive app for Mac, or Windows personal computers here:

https://www.google.com/intl/en_US/drive/start/download.html

When Google Drive first runs on your personal computer it asks you to sign-in to your Google Account. This links that Drive app to that account. Any computer signed-in to that Google Account will have access to the contents of that Drive. So, you can put a file into your Drive on one computer and then take it out on another computer.

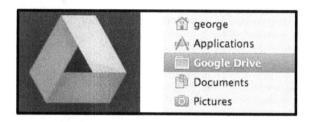

On your personal computer, Google Drive is composed of two parts: the Google Drive app which you have to download and install just like any other app (see the link above) and a "Google Drive Folder" representing your storage space on the Google servers. The icons for this app and folder on my Macintosh are shown in this figure.

The "Google Drive Folder" isn't really a folder, it just acts like one. You can drag files into or out of this "Google Drive Folder" just as if it were a real folder in your personal computer file system. If you drag a file into the "Google Drive Folder" it is actually sent off to the Google servers somewhere in the cloud and a link to that file is stored in the folder on your personal computer. If you drag a file out of this "Google Drive Folder" it is sent back to your personal computer and removed from the Google servers. The "Google Drive Folder" is installed at the same level in your personal computer file system as your "Documents" folder on a Mac.

So, when you "Upload" a file from your Nexus-7 to your Google Drive, you will find that file inside the Google Drive folder on your personal computer as illustrated in this screenshot taken from my Macintosh. As I mentioned above, you can drag files into or out of your Google Drive folder on your personal computer and those changes will be reflected back to the Google Drive servers and thence to your Nexus-7.

7.4 -Google Drive Using a Web Browser

You can access your Google Drive using any internet connected computer that has a web browser installed. You might have to use this technique if you are using someone else's computer - for example at a hotel - and you cannot install the Google Drive app as discussed in the last section.

Using any web browser, go to: https://drive.google.com/#my-drive

After signing-in to your Google Account, you will see the contents of the Google Drive associated with that account as illustrated below. In this figure, my Drive contains the "My First Spreadsheet" and the "My First Doc" files that I created on my Nexus-7 way back in Section 7.2.1

For this example, I am using the Chrome web browser. If you are not using the Chrome Browser on your personal computer, you should be.

This figure illustrates a new feature of Google Drive. At the right of the figure is a listing of all the recent activity on my Drive. This is not particularly interesting if you are the only person who uses this Drive, but if you are collaborating with a work group on a document, for example, it might be very helpful to have a "paper trail" of all the recent changes to that file and who made them.

7.4.1 - Working with Google Documents using a Web Browser

To open a file or folder simply click on its name in the list. For example, clicking the "My First Doc" file in the figure above, opened that file as illustrated in the figure to the left. I could now make changes to it or continue typing more content. Once again, any changes made will be instantly (almost) saved to your Google Drive on Google servers. You never have to "save" a Google Document file. You never have to back up that file. Google does it all automatically. Really slick!

Another way to perform various actions on a file in your Google Drive from a web browser is first to select the file by clicking the checkbox just to the left of the file name and then clicking on the "More" menu icon as illustrated in this figure.

That will drop down a menu with several actions that you can apply to the selected file. These include Opening it, Renaming it, Downloading it from the Google servers, or Removing it from your Google Drive.

Remember that documents created in Google Drive are "native" Google format files. Only Google Drive can create or edit them. So, if you want to download a native Google document file, such as "My First Spreadsheet" in the illustration above, you will not be able to edit it using any application on your personal computer. So, when you download one of these native Google document files, you are given the opportunity to convert the downloaded file into a format that you can edit with apps that you might have on your

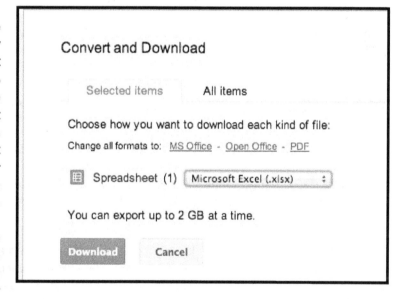

personal computer - MS Office file format for example. This is illustrated in this figure. In the case of my spreadsheet file, I have the choice of downloading it as an MS Office (Excel) file, an Open Office file or as a non-editable PDF file. Open Office is a free app that can open and save MS Office documents. If you are not using the heavy-lifting capabilities of MS Office, you might save yourself some money, and frustration, by trying out Open Office.

Although it is done all the time, it is incredibly rude to send someone an MS Office formatted file. You are assuming that they own MS Office, else they wouldn't be able to open the file you sent. It is much more polite to send a universally readable file format such as PDF. That's why PDF files were invented. So, if you want to send your file to someone and you are not positive that they own the proper app to open it, send it as a PDF file - the last option in the dialog above. Everyone can open PDF files. There, that's my sermon for today.

7.4.2 - Uploading Files from Your Personal Computer

In the previous section I discussed downloading Google Drive files to your personal computer. In this section I will discuss the opposite - uploading files from your personal computer to your Google Drive using a web browser.

The figure at the start of Section 7.4, illustrates what the Google Drive window looks like when accessed from a web browser. Near the upper-left corner of that figure is a big red "Create" button. I have reproduced that portion of the Google Drive window here at the left. Next to the "Create" button is a button that looks like an arrow pointing upwards out of a hard drive. Clicking on that button will upload a file or a folder from your personal computer's file system into your Google Drive using the web browser interface.

Clicking on the Upload button opens the brief menu giving you the option of uploading "Files" or "Folder..." as shown outlined in the figure. Clicking on the "Files..." opens a file browser window that, on my Macintosh, looks like the figure at the right. The file I have outlined, "Chrome Book Description" is an MS Word (.docx) file. Clicking on this file starts the Upload process. During that process, the Word format file is converted into a Google Doc format file so that it can be edited in Google Drive using your Nexus-7.

Uploading an MS Office type file actually results in two files being saved to your Google Drive as illustrated at the right. The first file is the original Office file, a docx file in this case. The second file is the original file converted to the corresponding Google Docs file type, gdoc in this case. It is this gdoc file that can be edited on your Nexus-7.

Google has recently purchased "QuickOffice" and has begun integrating it into Google Drive. This will give Nexus-7 users the ability to work directly with Microsoft Office files without having to convert them into Google Docs formats. Until then, when uploading files from your personal computer to Google Drive, your "Office-like" files will be converted to their corresponding Google file types: Word files -> Google Docs files; Excel files -> Google Sheets files; PowerPoint files -> Google Slides files. You need to do this if you want to be able to open and work on these files using Google apps on your Nexus-7.

At this time, Google cannot convert the Macintosh Pages, Numbers, or KeyNote file types. If you do upload one of these files, it will be uploaded in its Mac file format (i.e. you will not be able to open it with Google apps). The work-around, at least until Google adds the functionality to convert Pages, Numbers, and Keynote files, is first to export those files on your Mac to the corresponding Office-like file types. So, for example, if you have a Numbers document that you would like to upload so that you can use Google Sheets to collaborate on its editing, you would first open the file in Numbers and then export it as an Excel file. You will be able to upload this file type to Google Drive and continue working on it with Google Sheets.

7.5 - Google Drive on Your Chromebook

Google "Chromebook" laptop computers are becoming more and more popular. They are built specifically to run the Chrome OS which is built upon the concept of cloud computing just as your Nexus-7 is. A Chromebook would make an ideal companion for your Nexus-7. As with the Nexus-7, Chromebooks are very inexpensive and powerful since they have the resources of Google behind them.

On a Chromebook, Google Drive is already installed and is represented by a Drive icon just as on your Nexus-7. When you click on this app icon, a window opens showing the contents of your Google Drive. This window looks and acts exactly the same as if you had accessed it using a web browser as described in Section 7.4. In reality, that's exactly what you did - remember, Chrome is basically a web browser and Chrome "apps" are really mostly links to websites. So, the Google Drive "app" on a Chromebook is just a link to the same website I gave you at the beginning of section 7.4. From there on the discussion is the same as in Section 7.4.

8 - Downloading to Your Nexus-7

In Chapter 7 we have been discussing uploading and downloading files between your Nexus-7 and your Google Drive. But there are other ways that files can be downloaded to your Nexus-7. I won't discuss downloading apps from the Google Play Store because that has already been discussed in Section 4.8. Three other ways that files can be downloaded to your Nexus-7 are:

1) As attachments to email messages   (Section 8.1)
2) As PDF files downloaded from web pages   (Section 8.2)
3) As images downloaded from web pages   (Section 8.3)

When you download a file by one of these means, it gets stored on your Nexus-7's built-in storage. You can access these downloaded files by using an app cleverly named "Downloads". The Downloads app icon looks like that at the right. You can find it pre-installed on you Nexus-7 on the "All Apps" screen.

8.1 - Downloading Email Attachments

The figure at the right illustrates a Gmail message I received with a photo attached. I might want to download this attached image file to my Nexus-7 so that I can do something with it - perhaps print it and hang it on my wall.

To download an email attachment to your "Downloads" app, just Touch the image in the email message.

That will open a screen as illustrated below. Touching the "3-squares" menu icon shown outlined in the upper-right corner of the figure drops down the menu as illustrated. Touching "Save" puts the file into your Downloads app.

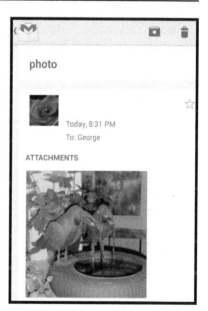

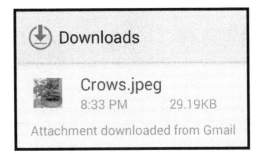

Launching the Downloads app confirms that the file has been saved to my Nexus-7. Touching the file name, "Crows.jpeg" in this case, opens the dialog below where you can choose what to do with the file.

You could print the image by selecting "Cloud Print". Or, you could open the image in any of the image editing apps installed on your Nexus-7. Opening the image file in the "Photos" app allows you to upload the file to your Google Drive as described in Section 7.2.3.

8.2 - Download a PDF File from a Web Page

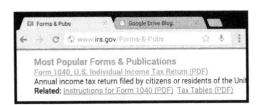

Some web pages provide links that allow you to download PDF files. For example, the IRS.gov website illustrated at the left allows you to download income tax forms in PDF file format. To download a PDF file to your Nexus-7's Downloads app, just Touch the link to the file on the webpage.

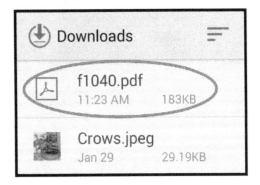

The file you Touched is downloaded and placed into your Downloads app. Touching the name of the downloaded file in Downloads will provide you a list of possible apps that can open that type of file. This is illustrated on the next page.

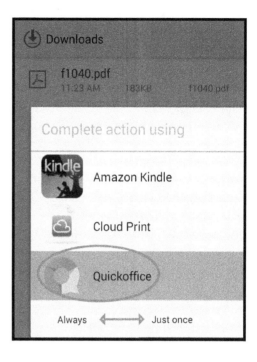

In this case, since I am trying to open a PDF file, my Nexus-7 is offering three apps that can handle that type of file. I could send the file to the Kindle Reader app installed on my Nexus-7 if it were a long document that I just wanted to read. Or I could print the PDF file by selecting "Cloud Print". In the case illustrated I have chosen to open the file using the "Quick Office" app. Notice that once I have selected which app to use to open this type of file, I can specify whether to use this app only for this specific file "Just Once" or for every file of this type I download in the future "Always".

8.3 - Download an Image from a Web Page

Sometimes you see an image on a webpage and would like to download it to your Nexus-7. As an example, I found this image of the new Red Nexus-5 phone on a Google website. To download an image that you see on a webpage, Touch and hold on the image.

That will open a menu of options as illustrated at the left. Touch "Save Image" and that will download the image file to your "Downloads" app as illustrated at the right.

9 - Nexus 7 Cameras

The Nexus-7 has two cameras. The "front facing" camera, i.e. the one facing your face, has only 1.2 mega-pixel and is fixed focus. It is intended for showing your face during video chats and "selfies". It is not a high quality camera as cameras go and you wouldn't want to use it to take pictures of your wedding. For more serious photography, the "rear facing" camera, the one that points away from your face, has 5 mega-pixel and automatic focus. It isn't a great camera as cameras go, but it is quite adequate for snapshots and the like.

For taking photographs, both cameras are controlled by an app cleverly named "Camera". You will find its icon on your Home Screen or on the "All Apps" screen. Touching the Camera icon takes over the Nexus-7 screen and converts it into the viewfinder for the currently active camera.

9.1 - Camera Controls

At the bottom of the Camera screen are three icons as illustrated at the right. The big blue circle in the center is the "shutter button". Touching it will take a picture. Pressing one of the volume buttons will also take a photo and may be easier.

You can force the camera to focus on a particular area in the scene by simply Touching the screen where you want the camera to focus. When you Touch the screen a symbol like this will appear where you touched. It may wiggle for a moment while the camera focuses. When the icons inside the circle turn green, the camera has acquired focus.

In the figure upper-right, the icon at the right, the one that looks like an empty circle. Is the Camera controls button. Touching this "empty circle" icon will reveal the Camera controls as shown in the figure below. Sometimes when you try to Touch a camera control, you end up taking a picture instead. It may be easier to Touch-and-Hold on the camera control icon until the controls appear and then slide your finger up to the control you want without lifting it off the screen. Continue Touching-and-Sliding until you reach the control you want and then lift your finger off the screen. You may want to experiment and see what technique works best for you.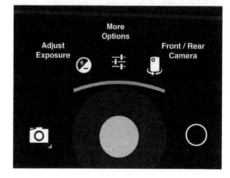

Touching the icon that I have labeled "Front / Rear Camera" toggles between using the front-facing, "selfie", camera and the rear-facing camera that you will use for photography. If you see your face on the screen, you are using the "selfie" camera. Just Touch the "Front / Rear" icon again to switch to the photography camera.

9.1.1 - Exposure Control

Touch-and-Hold on the "Adjust Exposure" icon in the previous figure to reveal a control, illustrated at the left that will allow you to adjust the camera exposure in 1-stop increments. Choosing a "+" number will make the photo lighter and Touching a "-" number will make it darker. You will see the result of these adjustments on the screen as you make them. Again, you may find it easier to Touch-and-Hold on the "Adjust Exposure" icon and then to Slide your finger up to the exposure number you want without lifting your finger off the screen. Experiment.

Touching the "More Options" icon shown in the middle of the figure on the previous page reveals a menu of options as illustrated at the right. Starting at the left:

9.1.2 - GPS Location

The "Location On/Off" icon toggles between recording the GPS location of each photo along with the actual image. This is incredibly useful for taking travel photos where you may not remember exactly where each photo was taken. If you are a secret agent and don't want your photo locations tracked, you might want to turn this service OFF. If the service is OFF, there will be a line across the Location icon. So, in this illustration, the Location service is ON.

9.1.3 - Countdown Timer

Touching the "Countdown Timer" icon brings up the dialog shown to the left where you can set a time delay between the time you Touch the shutter button and when the photo is actually take. This is useful if you need to run around and get in the photo yourself.

9.1.4 - Picture Size

Touching the "Picture Size" icon in the "More Options" display brings up this menu of possible "picture sizes". Actually, "picture size" is a misnomer since the pictures are actually all the same "size" for the 5M, the 3M, and the 2M options. What these options change is the "resolution" of the photos - how many pixels are contained within the photo. This changes the file size needed to store the image, but it does not change the "size" of the photo itself.

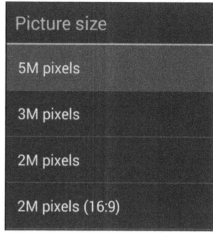

The only option shown that actually changes the picture size is the "2M pixels (16:9)" option. The other photos all have a 4:3 "aspect ratio" which matches the screen used for "old fashioned" TV sets. The 16:9 aspect ratio option cuts off the top and bottom of the image to make it fit properly on a modern TV wide screen display which also has a 16:9 aspect ratio.

If you are confused by all this, don't worry. Just leave this setting on "5M pixels" That will capture the most detail possible with this camera. If you know that you will only be displaying your photos on a 16:9 TV screen, then choose the 16:9 option here. But, keep in mind that if you ever want to print your photos on real paper, the 5M option will yield the best results.

9.1.5 - Color Balance

Sorry, I have called this control "Color Balance" whereas Google calls it "White Balance". It's the same thing. The idea here is that the apparent color of objects changes depending upon the color of the light that is illuminating them. Incandescent light is "orange". Fluorescent light is "green". Sunny light is "white", and Cloudy light is "blue".

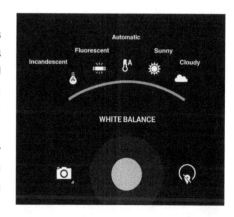

So, if you don't want your photos to come out orange, or green, or blue, you can fix those colors by selecting the type of light you will be shooting your photos in. Or, just set it on "Automatic" and let the Nexus engineers worry about it.

9.1.6 - Scene Mode - Labeled "SCE" in the More Options Menu

This menu lets you set several camera parameters to best match the type of scene you are shooting. For example, "Action" will prefer a fast shutter speed. "Night" will increase the camera's sensitivity for low light levels. And so forth. I have no idea what settings "Party" favors. You can probably leave this setting on "None" and just let the camera figure out what it wants to do.

9.1.7 - Camera Modes

At the bottom-left of the figure just above is an icon that looks like a camera. Touching this icon opens the menu illustrated in the figure below where you can choose various camera modes.

Single Shot:

The mode you will probably use most often is the "Single Shot" mode we have been discussing up until now. Touch the blue Shutter Button or one of the volume buttons to take a photo.

Videos:

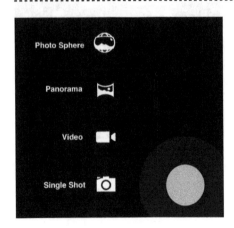

The Nexus-7 can also take videos. Just Touch the Video Camera icon. When you do that, the "Shutter Button" turns to red from blue so that you can quickly tell which mode you are in. Touch the red button to start and again to stop the recording.

Please Note: You **MUST** hold the Nexus-7 in landscape mode when shooting a video. Remember you are going to watch it on a TV set. So, unless you plan on turning your TV set on its end, hold the camera in the same orientation as the TV set.

Panorama:

When you select the Panorama Mode, the Nexus-7 display will look something like this. You will actually see the scene that you are pointing the camera at, but I have placed a lens cap over the lens of my Nexus-7 to make these screenshots clearer.

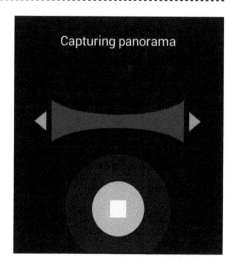

You are going to be taking a very wide shot of the scene by sweeping the camera sideways across the scene while the image is being exposed. Touch the Shutter Button to start the process. The Button will change into a "Stop" Button as shown in this figure. Touch "Stop" to interrupt the process.

When you Touch the Shutter Button, you will be prompted to start sweeping the camera across the scene in either direction indicated by the arrows at the two ends of the panorama icon.

Photo Sphere:

Photo Sphere is the last camera mode and it is, to the best of my knowledge, unique to Google. The idea is that you are going to capture a series of shots pointing in various directions all around and above where you are standing. This is very much like the Google "Street View" cameras that drive all around the world so that you can see everything without leaving home.

When you select Photo Sphere Mode, you will see a display something like the figure to the right. Of course, you will see the scene rather than a black screen. Hold the camera

vertically in portrait mode. What you have to do is move the camera so that the white dots that appear on the scene are in the center of the "Bull's Eye". When you have the dot aligned inside the Bull's Eye, the photo will be taken automatically and another series of dots will appear as illustrated at the left. Just keep moving the Bull's Eye to one of the dots until no more dots appear. You are done. Here's how Google suggests you work:

"Slowly rotate around keeping your Nexus-7 as close to your body as possible while still being able to see the screen. Capture photos around the horizon first. Then, slightly tilt the camera up or down, keeping your Nexus-7 roughly in the same location. Repeat the above process to capture several rows of photos (most devices will require five rows for a full sphere)".

9.1.8 - Viewing Your Last Shot

Regardless of what type of shot you have just taken, single shot, video, etc, the method for viewing it is the same. Swipe left from just off the right side of the screen. That will reveal the last shot you took. Swipe again and you will move back through all of the shots you have taken. Swipe back to the right to move the photos off the screen and you will end up back at the camera.

10 - Importing Photos

Your Nexus-7 is not the only camera you may own, and from time to time you might want to import photos from your "real" camera into your Nexus-7. To do this you will need to purchase some hardware and a media importing app from the Google Play Store. All this is explained in this chapter.

10.1 - Using a microUSB to SD Card Adaptor

Most digital cameras record their photos on an "SD Card" ("SD" stands for "Secure Digital", but that name is almost never used). The easiest way to import your photos is to remove the SD card from your camera and plug it into the microUSB port on the bottom of your Nexus-7. You will immediately notice that it is impossible to plug an SD card into a microUSB port. So, the first thing you will need is an adaptor into which you can plug the SD card. The second thing you will need is an app that allows you to transfer the image files from the SD card to your Nexus-7's internal storage. I will discuss that in the next section.

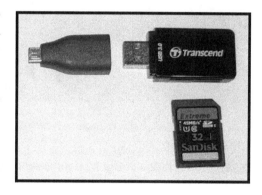

For this example I purchased a "StarTech Micro USB OTG to USB Adaptor" ($6.73 from Amazon) and a "Transcend Information USB 3.0 Card Reader (TS-RDF5K)" ($7.22 from Amazon). These are shown along with an SD Card from my camera in this figure. The "OTG" in the name of the USB adaptor is apparently quite important. It means "On the Go", which makes it different from a not-OTG adaptor in some obscure way. In order to work with the Nexus-7 the adaptor must be "OTG". As indicated in the figure, the SD card from your camera plugs into the SD Card reader which plugs into the USB adaptor and the whole assembly plugs into the micro-USB port on the bottom of your Nexus-7. Be careful, the microUSB connector is fragile and it plugs in in only one way.

Before you can import images from the camera SD card, you will need an app for that.

10.2 - Installing the Nexus Media Importer App

The Nexus Media Importer app is available from the Google Play Store for $3.99 and is essential to allow importing photos from an external SD card.

10.3 - Importing Photos from Your Camera's SD Card

When you first launch the Nexus Media Importer app, it will tell you that it can now write files to your external SD card as well as read them and then take you to this dialog where you allow the app to access the SD card. Check the "Use by default" box and you won't see this dialog again.

That will take you to this dialog where you will Touch the "Photos" category to import photos from the SD card. There are other types of files that Media Importer can handle, such as Music and Videos, but I have not shown them in this figure.

You finally arrive at the screen at the left which shows a list of all the photos stored on the external SD card. This entire display appears after you have selected a photo from the list. The idea here is that you select a photo from the list on the left, and then perform some action on that photo by touching the various buttons shown mostly along the upper row in the figure.

The first button to notice is this one which coverts to a full-screen display. You can also enter full screen mode by double-tapping on a photo. You will see a single photo filling the screen and you can go from photo to photo by swiping across the screen to the left or right. This is perhaps the easiest way to browse through your photos. You can zoom in to examine a photo in detail by Touching-and-Holding on it. You can then zoom in or out using the pinch gestures. Double-tap to zoom back to the original full screen display size. Double-tap on the photo again and that will take you back to the main display shown above left. You can use the swiping left or right gesture to move between photos in this display without going to the full screen display if you prefer.

When you have selected a photo to act on, attention shifts to the row of action icons along the top of the screen.

The first two icons are the "Copy" and "Move" icons illustrated at the right. Touching the first icon "Copies" the selected photo to the Nexus-7 internal storage. "Copy" means that the original file is left on the SD card. The second icon is the "Move" icon and this moves the file from the SD card to the Nexus-7's internal storage. The file is no longer on the SD card.

The "Trash Can" icon should be self explanatory. It deletes the photo from the SD card. I would experiment with an SD card from your camera before choosing either "Trash Can" or "Move" icons since these make changes to the SD card itself. Make sure that these changes leave the SD card in a state that is still compatible with your camera before you perform these actions on an "important" camera card.

Up to this point we have been talking about selecting a single photo. This could be tedious if you want to import a lot of photos. Media Importer has a solution for that. Touching the menu icon in the upper-right corner drops down a menu, a portion of which looks like the illustration at the right. The "Select Mode" item shows that the current mode is to select a single

photo. Touch that menu item and that will reveal another menu as illustrated at the left where you can choose "Multiple" or "Range" selection modes as well as Single.

"Multiple" mode lets you select multiple photos by Touching each one you want to select. They don't have to be contiguous. If you Touch the wrong photo, just Touch it again to de-select it.

At the bottom of the figure is a third Select Mode called "Range". This mode allows you to Touch a photo at the start of a range of photos you want to select, and then scroll to the end of that range and Touch the last photo in that range. That selects all the photos between the first and last photos you Touched.

Even with Multiple and Range modes, it would still be cumbersome to import all of the photos on an SD card. So, when you are in either the "Multiple" or "Range" modes, the menu changes to include an item "Select New/All". This allows you to quickly select All of the photos on the SD card, or only those that are "New", i.e. that aren't already in your Nexus-7's internal storage.

OK. At this point we have selected all of the photos we want to import.

Where's the "Import" button? There isn't any. Instead, Media Importer provides a "Share" button as illustrated at the left. Touching this button allows you to import the selected photos or to share them in several different ways as illustrated on the next page.

These are just some of the possible ways to share the photos from your camera's SD card. The whole menu has even more possibilities.

Touch "Drive" and your selected photos will be transferred to your Google Drive

Touch "Gmail" and a new message will be created with your selected photos attached.

Touch "Google+" and you will be able to share your photos with "Friends" "Family" or any other of your Google+ "Circles".

Touch "Hangouts" and you can share your photos as part of a Google+ chat or video conference session.

And lastly, in this illustration at least, if you Touch "Photos" the photos from your camera's SD card will be imported into the "Photos" app on your Nexus-7.

And, finally, the photo I had selected and "Shared" to my "Photos" app is there inside the "Pictures" Folder as illustrated at the right.

So, we now know how to take photos with the Nexus-7's camera and we know how to import photos taken with a "real" external camera. Now, what can we do with these photos?

11 - Working with Photos

As I have mentioned previously, there are two apps on your Nexus-7 that work with photos. They are named "Photos" and "Gallery". I expect that eventually one or the other of these will be eliminated or merged into a single app. But for right now, I will discuss both in this chapter.

Just to make the situation even more complicated, Google provides a third option for working with your photos. It is a web based app that is part of Google+. I will also discuss this option.

11.1 - Using the "Photos" App

The "Photos" app is pre-installed on your Nexus-7. Images that you download from the internet or receive as email attachments, photos that you take with the Nexus-7's built-in camera, photos that you import from an external camera's SD card, and screen shots that you take of your Nexus-7's screen will all appear in the "Photos" app.

So, now that you have all those photos in "Photos", what can you do with them?

To get started, launch the Photos app by Touching its icon illustrated just above. It will be on your Home Screen or the All Apps Screen.

This is a portion of the first screen you will see when you launch the Photos app for the first time. This menu allows you to choose to see photos and videos that have been organized in various ways. For example, the "Google+" item takes you to photos that you have uploaded to your Google+ account. Other items below the portion I have shown allow you to see "Photos of You", Videos, Photo Albums you may have created, and photos that you have uploaded to Google+ that have received the "Auto Awesome" treatment. I will let you explore these on your own.

For now, Touching the "Photos" item shown outlined will take you to the photos that have been stored in the Photos app on your Nexus-7.

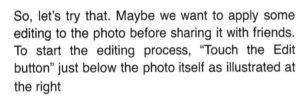

And here we are. This is the photo that we transferred from the external camera SD card to the Nexus-7's Photos app in Section 10.3.

Touching a photo on the screen shown at the left will open that photo in its own window as illustrated directly below. Notice that, along the lower edge of this figure, there are three virtual buttons that I have labeled "Edit", "Share", and "Delete". These labels do not appear on the Nexus-7 itself. So, when I say "Touch the Edit button", you will understand that you will really Touch the icon that looks like a paintbrush.

So, let's try that. Maybe we want to apply some editing to the photo before sharing it with friends. To start the editing process, "Touch the Edit button" just below the photo itself as illustrated at the right

11.1.1- Editing Photos with "Photos"

Touching the "Edit" button will open the editing window illustrated at the left. Notice that there are now three virtual buttons along the bottom edge of the window labeled "Rotate", "Crop", and "Filters". These labels actually do appear on the Nexus-7 screen.

Rotate:

Touching the "Rotate" button rotates the photo 90° clockwise. This is nice because it makes better use of the Nexus-7 display - the photo appears bigger so more detail is visible. Touching "Rotate" three more times will return the photo to its original orientation.

When making any edit of your photo, there will be two virtual buttons somewhere on the screen that I have not shown in these illustrations. These buttons are "Save" and "Cancel". It you like your edit and want to keep it, Touch "Save". If you're sorry you ever started with this edit, Touch "Cancel".

Crop:

The next edit button is "Crop". Touching "Crop" opens this window where you have three options for cropping your photo.

The first option is "Free". That means that you are free to crop the photo any way you want to. Just Touch-and-Drag the handles that appear so that only that portion of the photo that you want to keep is inside the white lines. Then Touch the "Save" button - it looks like a check mark.

The middle cropping option is "Original". This option allows you to change the size of the cropping window, but the aspect ratio of the cropping window will remain the same as that of the original photo. So, if your original photo had an aspect ratio of 4:3, your cropped photo will also.

The third cropping option is "Square". The cropped photo will be square. This is the option I have illustrated in the figure above. Some photo sharing sites like square photos and this is how to make them.

The third editing option is labeled "Filters" as shown in the illustration at the upper-right of this page. Touching the "Filters" button actually allows you to apply two types of edits to your photo. The first actually is "Filters" and the second is "Frames". Both of these are illustrated on the next page.

Filters:

Touching the "Filters" edit button opens this screen. Notice that along the bottom of this screen are two options labeled "Filters" and Frames".

The "Filters" option opens a window like this one. Arrayed along the bottom are several different filters that you can apply to your photo: "Warm", "Cross", "B&W", "Cool" and so forth. When you Touch one of these filter buttons, that filter will be applied to your photo. It may also reveal a row of dots as shown just above the label "Cool" in this illustration. That row of dots indicates that there is more than one version of this filter. Touch again and you will see the next version. Keep Touching and you will cycle through all of the versions.

Frames:

Not much to say here. Touch "Frames" and select a frame for your photo. That's about all there is to it.

Remember to Touch "Save" (the check mark) whenever you make an edit.

A/B Testing:

When you perform an edit on your photo, you will see an icon that looks like this in the upper-right corner of the screen. Touch-and-Hold this icon and you will see the original photo. Release this icon and you will see the edited version.

11.1.2 - Sharing Photos from "Photos":

Once you have edited your photo to your satisfaction, you might want to share it with other people. To start the sharing process, Touch the "Share" icon at the bottom of the window that opens when you select a photo. This is illustrated a couple of pages back just above the Section 11.1.1 label.

When you Touch the Share button, you are choosing to share the current photo. A portion of the window that opens is shown in this figure which shows six different ways you can share your photo. But there are about a dozen and the number will depend upon which "social apps" you have installed on your Nexus-7.

The top row of potential sharing targets are links to Google+. Google+ is Google's version of Facebook. It is huge and getting bigger every day. Google is integrating more and more of its services into Google+. Touching one of these buttons will share your photo with people, groups of people (Circles) or with everyone (Public). If you would like to learn more about Google+, I have written a book titled "Introduction to Google+" that is available from the Amazon Book Store.

Touching the "People" button will take you to a page listing all of the people you have added to your Google+ account as well as everyone in your Nexus-7 "People" contacts book. Touch the person you want to share this photo with and Touch "Done" in the upper-right corner.

That will create a screen similar to the one at the right. There is a space for you to add a message. You can also add more photos by Touching the "Add More" button in the lower-left corner. When you're done, Touch "Share" in the upper-right corner and your photo(s) will be sent to your chosen recipient(s).

NOTE: This may look like an email message, but it is not. The photo will not be sent to your recipient via email. It is sent to that person's Google+ account. The next time that person signs-in to his/her account, they will see it. This means that in order to share a photo with someone by this method, that person must have a Google+ account.

This is what your recipient will see when they open their Google+ account.

If you want to share your photo with someone who doesn't use Google+, then it would be best to use some other method for sharing such as the "Gmail" sharing option shown in the figure on the previous page. Your photo will be sent as an attachment to a Gmail message.

OK, we have explored most of the features of the "Photos" app for storing, importing, editing, and sharing your photos. But, there is a second app provided by the Nexus-7 for dealing with photos. It's called the "Gallery" app and I will discuss it next.

11.2 - Using the "Gallery" App

Gallery

The Gallery app has many of the same capabilities as the "Photos" app and a few that Photos doesn't. All in all, Gallery seems to offer more "real" photography features.

Touching the Gallery app icon on your Home Screen or All Apps screen will open the app to a window like that shown at the right. This

example shows that there is a "Pictures" Album in Gallery and that it contains two photos. In this case, one of the two pictures in the album is the same one we have been using while discussing the Photos app. I didn't do anything to "move" this photo from the Photos app to the Gallery app. All of the photos stored on the Nexus-7 are available to both apps.

This figure shows one difference between the Photos and the Gallery apps. The Gallery app can open the Camera app by Touching the camera icon shown outlined in this figure. So, you can add photos you take with the Nexus-7 camera right from within the Gallery app.

Touching the "Pictures" Album shown in the previous figure opens a window showing the contents of that Album. Then, Touching one of the photos in the Album opens that photo in a window similar to that at the right.

The choices here are either to "Edit" the photo (lower-left corner) or to "Share" it (upper-right corner). The words "Edit" and "Share" do not appear on the Nexus-7 screen. I added them for clarity. I will discuss sharing photos later. Right now, let's take a look at what Gallery can do to Edit your photo. Touch the "Edit" icon that looks like a pencil.

11.2.1 - Editing Photos with Gallery

When the editing window opens, as illustrated at the left, there is a row of four icons along the bottom edge that represent the four types of editing Gallery can perform. Once again I have added the words for clarity.

The four types of edits that Gallery can perform are:

❖ Filters
❖ Frames
❖ Crop
❖ Effects (FX)

The Filters and Frames edit modes are basically the same as they were in the Photos app, so I won't go over them again here.

Crop:

The "Crop" edit in Gallery has two capabilities that the Photos app does not. One of them is the ability to rotate the photo to straighten photos that may have horizon lines or some other vertical or horizontal features in them that look "crooked" in the original. This is illustrated in the figure to the right.

The second "Crop" edit that Gallery can do that Photos cannot is to "Mirror" the image - to reverse it right to left. Sometimes this will yield a more pleasing composition. I have not illustrated that here, it's pretty obvious, but the icon to Touch is the last one in this figure, and in this case, the word "Mirror" actually does appear on the Nexus-7 screen.

11.2.2 - Gallery "Effects" Editing

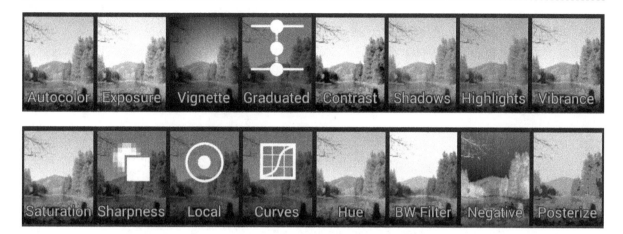

First let me make this perfectly clear: the name "Effects" is my own. I don't know what Google calls these edits. Some apps call them "Adjustments", but that word is too long for me to type, so I have chosen the word "Effects" with the abbreviation "FX" as the name for this category of edits.

The "Effects" editing category is the powerhouse of the Gallery app. There are 16 different ways to edit your photos included in the FX category. The icons and names for these edits are shown in the figure above. Many of these are common enough that I will not discuss them. For example, "Contrast", "Shadows", and "Highlights" are commonly available in photo editing apps like Photoshop Express, iPhoto, Lightroom, and others.

However, the Effects editing category offers three types of edits that are not so commonly available and that the Photos app cannot perform and I will discuss these three briefly in the following sections.

Vignette:

This figure illustrates the Vignette editing window. In case you can't tell from this figure, "Vignetting" darkens the corners of an image making the center stand out. This illustration is a bit extreme. The effect should be subtle enough that it might not be noticed, but I wanted to be sure that you noticed it here.

You can change the size and shape of the vignetting oval by dragging the handles attached to the oval. You then adjust the amount of vignetting, i.e. the amount of darkening, by dragging the slider at the bottom of the window. All of the Gallery editing windows have a slider to adjust the strength of the effect.

Once you have an effect that you like, Touch the checkmark at the right side of the window to save your edit. If you don't like anything this effect does, Touch the "X" at the left side to cancel this adjustment.

The Vignette edit can do more than just darken the areas outside the vignetting oval. Touching the word "Vignette" just below the slider in the previous figure reveals a pop up menu such as illustrated at the right that lists four different types of vignetting that Gallery can perform. I'll let you experiment for yourself to discover what the "Falloff", "Contrast", and "Saturation" vignette edits do.

Graduated:

It frequently happens when you take a photo that includes the sky that the sky comes out too light compared to the rest of the photo. This often leads to a washed out look to the sky. The "Graduated" FX edit lets you darken the sky in your photos. You can, of course, darken anything but this edit is most commonly applied to overexposed skies.

To use this effect, first drag the handles (the three dots) shown in this figure to adjust the location, the size, and the angle of the effect you want to create. It isn't apparent in this figure, but the effect doesn't have to be parallel to the top of the photo.

Once you have the location of the effect set, you can adjust the amount of darkening by dragging the slider. You can actually reverse the effect to brighten a dark area, for example an underexposed foreground, by dragging the slider farther to the right.

Local:

"Local" is a blockbuster effect. A while ago, Google bought a company named "NIK" that had developed a suite of powerful photo editing apps. That suite of apps cost around $500. Google now sells that same suite for around $150. "Local" is one of the editing effects from that suite and it is available "free" on your Nexus-7.

As you can see in this figure, there is a circle with handles so that you can adjust the location and the size of the circle. To operate "Local" you first place the center of the circle on an object in the photo. Then you adjust the size of the circle. When you perform these two operations, you are giving Local an instruction to "find everything inside this circle that "looks like" what I have placed the center of the circle on".

Local uses proprietary algorithms to figure out what "looks like" means and does an uncanny job of selecting similar objects inside the circle. These algorithms use characteristics such as color, contrast, structure, and others to define "looks like" objects. As you drag the circle around the image, Local shows those portions of the photo that it thinks "look like" what you have placed the center of the circle on by coloring them bright red. This may be hard to describe, but it's easy to see.

Here's an example that may help clarify what I'm trying to say:

I hope that you can see that Local has allowed me to change the brightness of the sky without changing the brightness of the trees or branches inside the circle. You may also notice that Local "feathers" the edges of the effect so that there are no abrupt edges in the resulting photo.

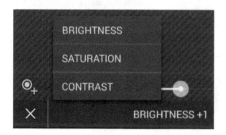

If you Touch the word "BRIGHTNESS" just below the slider, a popup menu will appear that allows you to choose whether to adjust Brightness, Saturation, or Contrast within the circle. Experiment. You may find some useful effects you can create using Local.

A/B Testing:

It is not apparent, but Gallery has an A/B testing capability as does the Photos app. It is just a little harder to find. There is no Edited/Original button as there is in Photos. Instead, when looking at an edited photo just swipe your finger in from the right or left edge of the photo. As your finger sweeps across the edited photo, the original photo will be revealed. This allows you to compare the edited vs the original version of the photo. Lift your finger off the screen and the edited photo will re-appear.

Return to the Original Version:

If you get all mixed up and just want to abandon your edits, Gallery has a way to do that. Touch the 3-squares menu icon in the upper-right corner of the Gallery screen and select "Reset". That will take you back to the original photo.

Saving Your Edits:

When you finish editing your photo, be sure to save the results. Just Touch the "Save" button in the upper-left corner of the editing screen as illustrated in the figure to the right.

11.2.2 - Sharing Photos from Gallery

Remember way back at the start of Section 11.2 there was a figure for which I said that there were two choices: "Edit" or "Share"? Well, we have now come to the "Share" part of the Gallery app.

When you have finished editing your photo and have "Saved" the result, you will be at a screen similar to the one illustrated at the left. You will also be at this screen if you choose a single photo from one of your photo albums.

There are two sharing options available as illustrated in the upper-right corner of the figure to the left. You will by now recognized the icon for your Google Drive. Touching this icon will send this photo to your Google Drive. Once the photo is in your Google Drive, you can access it from any computer in the world.

An extensive list of sharing options is revealed by Touching the "Share" button which is shown outlined in the figure. It is just to the left of the Google Drive icon. Touching the "Share" button drops down a long list of possible ways to share your photo as illustrated in this figure.

Touching "Google+" lets you share your photo with anyone who has a Google+ account.

Touching "Hangouts" lets you share your photo as part of a text or video chat. If you would like to learn more about Google+ or Hangouts, I have written a book titled "Introduction to Google+" that is available from the Amazon Book Store.

"Email" and "Gmail" let you send your photo to anyone as an attachment to an email message.

If you have installed the Facebook app on your Nexus-7, then you can share your photo with your Facebook friends as illustrated in the figure.

12 - Google+ Your Photos

Taking and sharing photos is an important part of the social networking experience and Google has made that easy, particularly as a part of Google+. Google+ is so important to the Google Empire, I have written a book titled "Introduction to Google+" that is available from the Amazon Book Store.

12.1 - Moving Photos to Your Google+ Account

Google+ offers an "Auto Backup" feature that automatically uploads your photos, as you take them, to your Goggle+ photo albums. If you would like to have your photos automatically backed up to your Google+ account, you have to enable that on your Nexus-7.

12.1.1 Enable Google+ Auto-Backup On Your Nexus-7

Launch the Google+ app on your Nexus-7. Touch the 3-squares menu icon in the upper-right corner of the screen and then Touch the Settings menu item as illustrated in the figure to the right. That will open a menu part of which is shown below. Touch the "Auto Backup: menu item.

And finally, that opens the long menu of settings for the Auto-Backup service illustrated at the right.

The first thing to do is to turn Auto-Backup ON by sliding the ON/OFF switch in the upper-right corner to the ON position. When it's ON, Auto-Backup sends every photo you take with your Nexus-7 camera and every screenshot you take "up" to the Google servers in the cloud. The photos use some of the storage space assigned to your Google Drive, but these photos do not appear in your Google Drive, They are accessible only via Google+. Auto-Backup will also, optionally, send every photo that is already on your Nexus-7 up to your Google+ Account. This all makes sense because Google+ is the hub of the Google "Sharing" Empire.

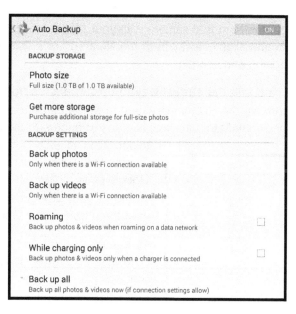

Starting at the top of the menu illustrated in the

figure is "Photo Size". This is very important because your choice here could ultimately cost you money. There are only two photo sizes to choose from: "Full Size" and "Standard Size". "Full Size" means that your Nexus-7 will send your photos in their original size. The storage space needed for your "Full Size" photos is charged against your Google Drive storage allocation - typically 15 GB of free storage. Beyond 15 GB you have to purchase additional storage space. So, you want to choose "Full Size" only if you really need it.

"Standard Size" means that Google will automatically re-size your photos so that the longest dimension is 2048 pixels or less. This is generally quite adequate for display on any TV or computer monitor. You can store an unlimited number of "Standard Size" photos in your Google+ Account at no charge.

The next few Auto-Backup Settings have to do with when you want the backups to occur. Generally your choice is: only when you have a WiFi connection or any time. Only when you are charging your Nexus-7 battery or anytime. When you are roaming for mobile data or not - hint: choose NOT.

The last item in the Settings menu is also important. "Backup All" means that your Nexus-7 will backup all the photos that are already stored on your Nexus-7 as well as any new ones that you take in the future. You will get a warning that if you choose "Backup All" it could take a long time depending upon how many photos you have on your Nexus-7.

Once you have your photos stored in your Google+ Account, you can access them from any computer in the world.

12.1.2 Uploading Photos from Your Camera to Google+

Uploading photos from your camera to Google+ is not strictly related to your Nexus-7. You will typically access your Google+ Account using your personal computer and not your Nexus-7. Still, I think it is important to know how your Nexus-7 fits into the bigger Google+ Empire. Google+ is where you will define who your "Friends" are, what groups of people you want to be able to see your photos, and many other aspects of "sharing". If you have a "real" camera, you may very well want to share photos from that camera with your friends as well as those you take with your Nexus-7. So I'm going to drift slightly away from the Nexus-7 for a little while to discuss the bigger world of Google+ photo editing and sharing.

I find that the easiest way to upload photos from my camera to my personal computer is simply to remove the SD memory card from the camera and insert it into the SD card slot on my Chromebook or on my Mac. One way to transfer photos to Google+ is first to transfer them into your Google Drive

folder. This is easy on your personal computer if you have installed the Google Drive app. Just drag the selected photos from the SD card into the Google Drive "folder" on your personal computer. Once you have your photos stored in your Google Drive, there is a Google+ Setting that allows you to view them from within Google+.

To enable viewing and editing of photos stored in your Google Drive folder from within Google+, go to the Google+ Settings page. To open your Google+ Settings page on your personal computer go to your Google+ Home Page and select the "Settings" item from the drop-down menu under the "Home" icon. "Settings" should be the last item in the list as shown at the left.

There are a lot of Google+ Settings. We are only interested in those pertaining to photos right now. Scroll down to the "Photos" settings as illustrated at the right. Check the Google Drive item so as to "Show Drive Photos in Your Photo Library".

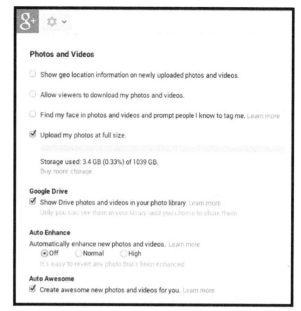

There are a couple of other things you might want to select or de-select in your Google+ Photos settings.

⦿ By default your photos are uploaded to Google+ at a maximum resolution of 2048 pixels on the longest side. If you would rather have them uploaded full size, then you want to check the box labeled "Upload my photos at full size". You can upload an unlimited number of default sized photos, but full size photos count against your allotted Google Drive storage space.

⦿ By default, all of your photos will be "Auto Enhanced" when they are uploaded to Google+. If you don't want this, set the "Auto Enhance" item to OFF. You can always Auto Enhance individual photos later.

⦿ By default, Google+ will create "Auto Awesome" photos for you automatically. If you don't want this to happen, un-click the "Auto Awesome" checkbox. There are six Auto Awesome effects that Google+ can create. Here's how Google describes them:

1) **Eraser** - If you take a sequence of 3 or more photos in front of a structure or landmark with movement in the foreground, Eraser will give you a photo with all the moving objects removed. It's helpful for those situations when you're trying to get a great shot of a landmark or other crowded place, but want to avoid including all of the people in the foreground of your photo.

2) **Action** - Take a series of photos of someone moving (dancing, running, jumping) and Auto Awesome will merge them together into one action shot where you can see the full range of movements in a single image, capturing the movement in one captivating still.

3) **Pano** - If you've taken a series of photos with overlapping landscape views, Auto Awesome will stitch these photos together into a panoramic image.

4) **HDR** - High Dynamic Range is the process of taking multiple exposures of the same image. By merging these images together, your photos will achieve a greater range of shadows and light. Uploading three similar images at different exposures--low, medium, and high exposure-- will create an HDR image for you.

5) **Motion** - If you've taken a series of photos in succession (at least 5), Auto Awesome will stitch these photos together into a short animation.

6) **Smile** - If you've taken a few group photos, Auto Awesome will choose the best shots of each person in your image and merge them into one great looking photo.

As you can see, some of these effects are what might be expected in a high priced photo editing app but with Google+ you have them free. "Auto-Awesome" in particular is almost like magic. Google recognizes what type of photo sequence you have uploaded, HDR or Panorama for example, and does the appropriate processing automatically.

12.2 - Editing Photos in Google+

In order to edit your photos in Google+, you must be using a Chrome OS device or the Chrome Browser on your personal computer. You cannot do this using Safari nor Internet Explorer.

To get started, open your Google+ Home Page and select "Photos" from the menu that drops down when you hover your cursor over the "Home" button in the upper-left corner. This will open a page, a portion of which is shown below. Here are the same photos we have been using all along on my Nexus-7, but now we are viewing them in Google+ on my personal computer.

Clicking on one of the photos on the screen shown at the right will open that photo in a window similar to that shown below.

In this window, we can perform simple editing such as cropping and rotating. But to access the entire set of powerful Google+ photo editing capabilities, click on the "Edit" button shown outlined in the figure to the left.

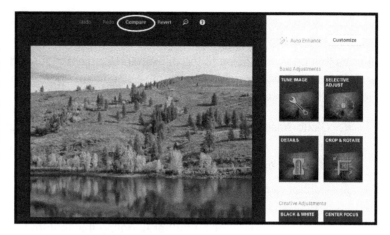

This illustrates the main Google+ photo editing window. There is an array of possible edits that can be performed on the selected photo arranged along the right side of the window. I have shown only the first four in this figure. There are another eight that I haven't shown.

A/B Testing

At the top of every editing window
is a button labeled "Compare" - shown outlined in the figure above. Clicking this button shows the original photo. Releasing the button shows the edited photo.

HDR Scape Editing Example

As an example, the figure at the right shows the "HDR Scape" editing window. This is typical of all the different types of editing that you can perform. At the top of the window are a series of "presets" for that type of edit. You can just click on one of these presets. Or, you can make your own adjustments by dragging the sliders back and forth.

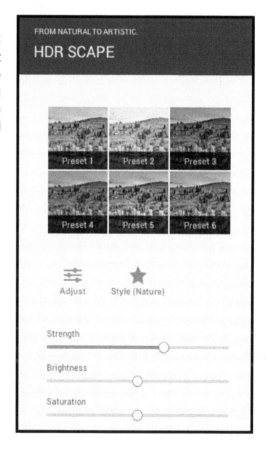

As an example, the two images at the left show the original (above) and the "HDR Scape" edited version (below) of our favorite photo.

12.2.1 - Late Breaking News: Google+ Photo Editing

Just as this book was going to the publisher, Google announced an update to Google+ version 4.3 for your Nexus-7. This update contains some significant updates to the photo editing portion of Google+. Some of these enhanced features include:

★ Cloud based photo editing: You can start editing a photo on one Chrome or Android device and then continue that editing on another device. All your changes, along with the original unedited version, are saved to Google servers.

★ Unified photo view: You will now be able to view all of your photos in one display. This includes all of your photos that are stored in the Google "cloud" and also those stored on your Nexus-7. Google will be further updating this feature to allow you to create folders to organize your photos sometime in the future.

★ Added editing features: The Google+ update for the Nexus-7 also includes some new photo editing features including "HDR Scape" which has been available on the web based version of Google+.

13 - Google Now

Google "Now" is a fairly new service that Google has built into your Nexus-7. The idea is that "Now" will provide you with information that you need or might like to have right "Now". And it does this without your having to ask for that information.

To activate "Now", just swipe your finger upward from the bottom of the screen as illustrated in the figure to the right. When you see the "Google" logo appear lift your finger off the screen and "Now" will appear.

This is an example of the type of information "Now" provides. In this example, "Now" displays a "Card" telling me that the New Balance running shoes that I ordered a couple of days ago have shipped and the expected arrival is on Saturday.

There is a "Card" that will provide me with more information about the Sochi Winter Olympics that are going on right now.

"Now" knows that I'm interested in the Nexus-7 and so it provides a Card with a link to news articles about Nexus related items.

Because "Now" knows where I am, it can tell me about the current weather.

Touching the link to more Nexus-7 information opens the screen illustrated on the right giving me up to date news about matters related to Nexus.

"Now" can provide a lot of timely information:

* It can display airline boarding passes.
* Remind you of upcoming meetings and events
* Display the current weather at your destination.
* Tell you when to leave home to get to the airport on time
* It can do currency conversions.

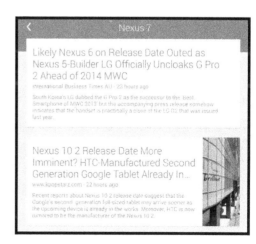

- Alert you to nearby attractions and events.
- Translate words from one language into another.
- Tell you when your bus is scheduled to arrive.
- Provide Zillow information about nearby real estate for sale.

And the list goes on. Google is adding new types of information that "Now" can provide every day. These types of information are called "Cards".

So, how does Google perform this magic? First, it knows where you are and what time it is at that location. So it can give you the current weather and tell you about nearby attractions. It knows what events are in your Google Calendar so it can remind you of upcoming items. But mostly Google can give you all this pertinent information because it reads your Gmail. When Amazon sends you an email confirming shipment of your order, Google recognizes what that message is and extracts the pertinent information. If your Dr sends you an email reminding you of your appointment, Google reads that reminder and extracts the pertinent information: time of the appointment, where it is, how long it will take you to get there, and so forth. If you buy airline tickets and the airline sends you a confirmation email, Google extracts the pertinent information such as flight number and date so that it can tell you when to leave for the airport and keep you up to date on any changes to your flights. It also "knows" where you're going so it can tell you about attractions there, give you directions to your hotel, translate "Hello" into the language at your destination. It seems like magic, but it is just Google doing its thing. If all this sounds creepy to you, you do have complete control over Google "Now" including the ability to turn it off completely.

13.1 - Google Now Settings

At the bottom of the "Now" screen is a 3-square menu icon as illustrated outlined in this figure. You may have to scroll down to the bottom of the screen to find it. Touching this menu icon and then the "Settings" item opens a menu of "Now" settings as illustrated in the figure below at the right.

As shown in the figure to the right there is an ON/OFF switch that allows you to turn "Now" OFF completely if you choose to. There are also other settings that you can adjust.

You can also leave "Now" ON but still control how individual Cards work. This is illustrated on the next page.

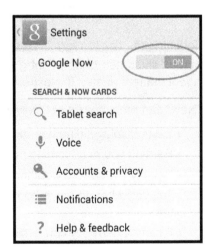

Near the upper right corner of each "Now" Card is another 3-square menu icon as illustrated here for the reminder about my running shoe delivery. Touching this menu icon will reveal a window where I can change how that type of Card works.

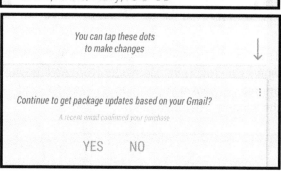

The figure to the right illustrates the window that opened when I Touched the 3-square menu icon in the figure above. In this case I can turn package tracking OFF by Touching the "NO" item.

The different types of Cards have different options that you can set. For example, the Card that tells you how long it is going to take you to get to a destination, the airport for example, gives you options for "Driving", "Walking", Biking", or "Public Transit". All Cards give you the option to turn that type of Card OFF.

Experiment with the different types of Cards to see what options they give you.

13.2 - Customizing Google Now

At the bottom of the Google "Now" screen there are three icons as illustrated here. You will probably have to scroll down to get to the bottom of the screen. We discussed the 3-square menu icon at the right side of this figure in the previous section. The middle icon shown outlined in this figure lets you customize "Now".

Touching the "magic wand" icon in the previous figure opens this window where you can customize "Now" to display things you are interested in. You can select the sports teams, and stocks, you want to follow. You can define places such as Home and Work so that "Now" can tell you how long it will take you to drive or walk to work with the current traffic conditions. You can tell "Now" what online video sources, such as NetFlix and Amazon Instant Video, you subscribe to. Basically, this is where you customize "Now" to give you the information you want without a lot of extraneous stuff you're not interested in.

13.3 - Google Now Reminders

The third icon at the bottom of the Google "Now" screen looks like a finger with a string wrapped around it and Touching that icon takes you to a screen where you can add Reminders to your "Now".

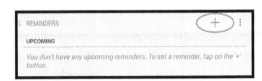

The figure at the right illustrates the window that opens when you Touch the Reminder icon. As it says, Touching the big "+" allows you to add a Reminder and that opens the window illustrated below.

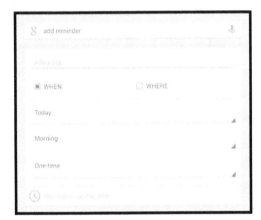

You can set the Reminder to remind you at a specific time, or at a specific location.

Touching the "WHEN" button as illustrated in the figure to the left, gives you the options to set "Today", "Morning", and "One Time". Each of these hides a short menu of other options. For example, Touching "Today", reveals the options: Today, Tomorrow, or on a specific date. Touching "Morning" reveals the options: Morning, Afternoon, Evening, Night, or "Set Time ..."

Touching the "One Time" item reveals a dialog as illustrated at the right where you can set up a repeating Reminder. You can set the Reminder to activate every Day, every Week, every Month, or annually.

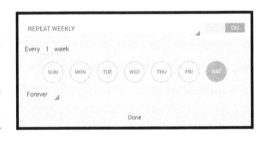

If you choose to repeat Weekly, you can select the day of the week as illustrated in the figure. If you choose to repeat Monthly, you can choose the day of the month, or to repeat on every occurrence of the day you are creating the Reminder. That means that if you are creating the Reminder on the 3rd Sunday of the month, you can set the Reminder to remind you on every 3rd Sunday.

And lastly, Touching "Forever" gives you the option to repeat the Reminder forever, or until a date in the future, or for a specific number of times.

Don't forget to give your Reminder a title at the top of the Reminder dialog. When you're done, Touch "Done" at the bottom of the dialog and you will be reminded.

14 - Connecting External Devices to Your Nexus-7

There are two primary ways in which you can connect external devices such as a keyboard, a mouse, or a hard drive, to your Nexus-7:

1) Using the microUSB connector port

2) Using Bluetooth

I will give a few examples in this chapter that should provide the information you need to connect other device to your Nexus-7. Not all devices will work, but the only way to find out is to try it out.

14.1 - Connecting a USB Mouse to Your Nexus-7

There's not much to say about connecting a USB Mouse to your Nexus-7. Just plug it in and it works. You have to use the "StarTech Micro USB OTG to USB Adaptor" ($6.73 from Amazon) that I described in Section 10.1. Plug the mouse USB connector into that adapter as illustrated in this figure and then plug the adaptor into the microUSB port on the bottom of your Nexus-7.

You can move the cursor around the screen and click to place an insertion point. Clicking the Mouse button is equivalent to Touching the screen with your finger. You can click-and-drag to select text. The mouse works pretty much as you would expect it to.

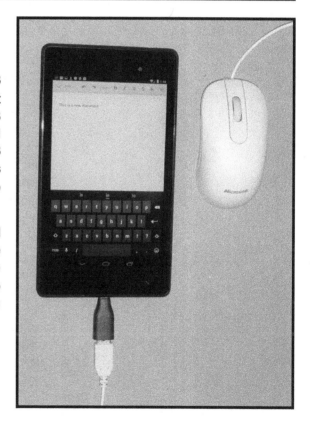

14.2 - Connecting a Bluetooth Keyboard to Your Nexus-7

This figure illustrates connecting an Apple wireless keyboard to a Nexus-7 using BlueTooth. Once connected, the keyboard works as expected. The best part is that the arrow keys on the keyboard can be used to move the insertion point in text which is much easier than trying to Touch the text in just the right spot.

To connect a BlueTooth device to your Nexus-7, you first have to turn BlueTooth ON. The easiest way to do this is to swipe down from the right half of the screen to reveal the "Quick Settings" menu as described in Section

4.10.2 and as illustrated in the figure on the right. Touch the "BlueTooth" item as shown outlined in the figure. That will take you to the actual BlueTooth Settings page illustrated in the figure below left.

Touch and slide the ON/OFF switch at the top of the screen to the ON position as illustrated. Now turn BlueTooth ON on the keyboard or other external device. The Nexus-7 will try for 2 minutes to find the keyboard. It may fail as it did when I tried this. If it fails to find your keyboard, turn BlueTooth back OFF on you Nexus-7 and then tune it back ON. If that doesn't work, turn BlueTooth on your keyboard OFF then back ON again. Keep trying.

Once your Nexus-7 and your keyboard find each other, you will get a "Pairing Request" as illustrated at the left. Type the 6-digit number displayed on the screen on your keyboard and hit Return or Enter. That will complete the pairing process and you should now be able to type on the BlueTooth keyboard anywhere the Nexus-7 virtual keyboard is displayed.

If you want to "un-pair" or rename a BlueTooth device, Touch the settings icon shown outlined in the figure to the right. There will be one of these for each BlueTooth device you have paired with your Nexus-7. The dialog that opens will allow you to give that device a different name or to "un-pair" it from your Nexus-7.

14.3 - Connecting an External Hard Drive to Your Nexus-7

The Nexus-7 comes equipped with either 16 or 32 GB Solid State Drives. In order to store a lot of "stuff" on your Nexus-7, you will have to resort to external storage of some sort. For modest quantities of "stuff" - an additional 16 or 32 GB for example - you can use an SD Card connected to the microUSB port on your Nexus-7 as described in Section 10.3. For larger quantities of storage, you can use an external hard drive connected to the same microUSB port using the same microUSB to USB OTG adaptor.

14.3.1 - Using an External Drive with Your Nexus-7

In order to find out just how this operates, I purchased a LaCie Porsche Design 500 GB USB 3.0 Mobile Drive - approximately $80 at Amazon. The LaCie 500 GB drive can be formatted for either Windows or Mac OS X file formats, but since the Nexus-7 recognizes only FAT32 (Windows) file formats, there is no need for the MAC OS X file support.

Formatting an External Drive

Right out of the box, the LaCie mobile drive is not recognized by the Nexus-7. The drive comes with formatting software that runs on Windows and Mac OS X computers, but not on Chrome computers.

So, before you can use an external drive with your Nexus-7, you will first have to connect the drive to either a Windows or Macintosh computer. Using the formatting app that comes with the LaCie drive, format the new drive as FAT32. You can give the drive a name. I used the name "External" in this example as shown in the figure to the right.

After formatting the drive as FAT32 using my Mac, I erased all of the LaCie files that were on the drive and created three folders named "Music", "PDF Files", and "Photos" as illustrated above. I then put six photo files into the "Photos" folder, a music file into the "Music" folder and a PDF file into the "PDF Files" folder. This is a simple example of using an external drive to store a large number of files that the Nexus-7's built-in memory is not large enough to hold.

Installing the Nexus Media Importer App

Before you can access files from an external drive, you will need an app for that. The Nexus Media Importer app is available from the Google Play Store for $3.99 and is essential to allow reading files from an external drive. "ES File Manager" is another highly rated file manager app.

Connecting an External Drive to Your Nexus-7

After formatting the external drive, I plugged it into my Nexus-7 using the same "StarTech Micro USB OTG to USB Adaptor" ($6.73 from Amazon) that I described in Section 10.1. The Nexus-7 provides power for the external drive through its microUSB port.

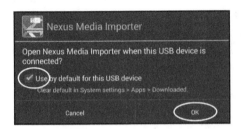

When an external drive is connected to the Nexus-7, the Nexus Media Importer app recognizes that event and launches itself automatically. You should see this dialog asking if you want to use the Media Importer app whenever this external drive is attached. Touch the check box and then OK.

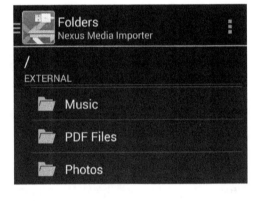

That will open the window illustrated at the right showing that there are three folders on the external drive. Actually, there are several other folders that I have not shown. The names for those files all start with a period ".". Files whose names start with a period are invisible on Macintosh computers. So, just pretend they are invisible here also. If you created the files and folders on a Windows machine, you may not see these additional folders.

To move forward through the Media Importer menu system, just Touch the item you want. To move backward, i.e. to go back to the page you just came from, Touch the three-horizontal-bar icon in the upper-left corner of the window. It's just to the left of the Media Importer icon.

Touching the "Music" folder name in the figure above will open a window such as the one illustrated at the left. For this example there is only one music file in the Music folder but you will probably have several more.

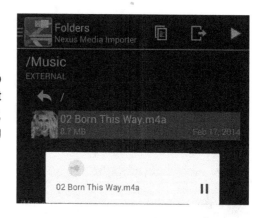

Touching the name of the music track that you want to play will open a window like the one at the right and that track will start playing. If it doesn't start automatically, Touching the "Play" icon (looks like a forward facing triangle) in the upper-right corner of the figure will start it.

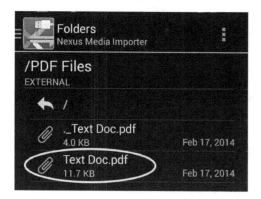

Touching the "PDF Files" folder name in the list of folders on the "External" drive as illustrated on the previous page will open a window such as is illustrated at the left. In this case I have not edited out the extraneous "._TextDoc..." file. Just ignore any file you see whose name starts with a ".".

Touching the name of the file, "TextDoc.pdf" in this example, will either open that file, or else it will open a dialog like the one illustrated just below.

This dialog is suggesting that you will have to download the chosen file to your Nexus-7 in order to find an app that can open it. You can choose to download it to the "Downloads" folder in which case it will be stored on your Nexus-7, or you can choose to download it "Temporarily" in which case it will not remain stored on your Nexus-7.

After downloading the pdf file, the Nexus-7 is suggesting that the Amazon Kindle app, or the QuickOffice app can open this type of file, or I could choose to print it by selecting "Cloud Print". I chose QuickOffice and that app opened the PDF file I created on my Mac and stored on the External drive as shown on the next page.

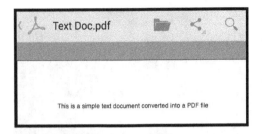

This is the PDF file I stored on the External drive using my Mac. The QuickOffice app on my Nexus-7 is able to open and share it.

The last folder I stored on the External drive is named "Photos". Touching that folder name in the list of folders shown two pages ago, opens this window showing all of the photos stored in the "Photos" folder on the External drive.

Touching the name of one of those photos opens that photo as illustrated. Using the icons shown along the upper edge of this figure, you can "Copy", "Move", Delete", or "Share" this photo. All of these icons and the operations they perform have been discussed previously in Section 10.3 so I won't do that again.

Transferring Files between an External Drive and Your Nexus-7

In the previous discussion we have been talking about using an external hard drive as an addition to the storage built-in to your Nexus-7. We have been leaving the files on the external drive and playing the music files or sharing the photo files directly from the external drive. You may also want to transfer files from an external drive to your Nexus-7's internal storage or to transfer files from your Nexus-7 to an external drive so as to make more space available on your internal storage. The Nexus Media Importer app can do both of these things.

Transferring files to or from an external drive is handled by the "Advanced" capabilities of the Nexus Media Importer. So, to start a file transfer, Touch the "Advanced" item at the bottom of the main Media Importer menu as illustrated at the left.

The figure at the right illustrates the main Media Importer "Advanced" screen. This screen is divided into two parts. The upper part shows files and folders stored on the External Drive. The bottom part shows files and folders that are stored in the Nexus-7's built-in memory. There are several more files that I have not included in these illustrations.

A basic rule when doing any file manipulations on your Nexus-7 is: "If you don't know what the file is or what it does, don't do anything to it!"

The basic idea when transferring files to or from your Nexus-7's internal storage is to select one or more files from the "From" file system and then select a folder from the "To" file system. In this example, I am going to copy a file from the Nexus-7's internal file system to a folder on the External Drive. This is illustrated in the figure to the right where I have begun navigating to the "from" file by Touching the "Pictures" folder in the Nexus-7 internal file system. The actual path to this folder is:

/storage/emulated/0/Pictures

Touching the "Pictures" folder in the previous figure opens this screen showing that the internal Pictures folder contains two sub-folders named "Photoshop Express" and "Screenshots". The file I want is the DSC03431 jpg file that resides in the "Pictures" folder itself. I have Touched the name of that file to select it as illustrated in the figure to the right.

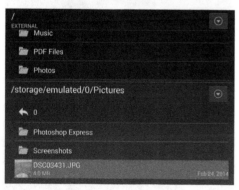

You can select one or more files by Touching each file name. You can de-select a file by Touching it again.

Having selected my "From" file, I now have to select my "To" destination folder. In this example I want to transfer the external file into the "Photos" folder in my Nexus-7's internal file system. So, I Touch the name "Photos" as illustrated in the figure to the left.

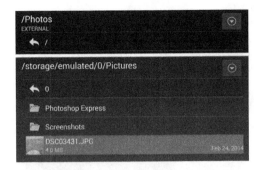

Touching the folder named "Photos" in the previous figure opens this screen illustrated at the left. This figure summarizes that I have selected the "Photos" folder in the External Drive and the DCS03431 file in the "Pictures" folder in the Nexus-7's internal; file system.

Having select both the "From" and the "To" items, we now have to perform the action.

To initiate an action on a selected file, Touch the downward pointing triangle in the upper-right corner of the portion of the file system window that contains the item to act upon. Both the internal and the external portions of the file system window have these downward arrows so be sure to use the one associated with the internal or the external file system that contains the file you want to act upon. In this example, I want to copy the DSC... file from the internal file system, so I have Touched the downward arrow shown outlined in the figure to the left.

Touching the appropriate downward pointing arrow reveals a pop-up menu as illustrated in the figure to the left. In this case, I want to "Copy" the file, i.e. I want it to remain in the internal file system and also to be copied to the External Drive file system. This is the action to take if you want to backup a file. IN that case you want the file to be stored in two different places. Selecting "Move" would delete the file from the internal file system. This would be appropriate if you wanted to free up some internal storage by moving file(s) to external storage.

After Touching "Copy" in the previous figure and confirming that I really do want to copy a file, the resulting file system looks like that in the figure to the left. Note that the DSC file has been copied to the External Drive as intended.

Navigating through the Nexus-7 file system is fairly straightforward. To see the contents of a folder, Touch the folder icon. To go back up one level in the file system, for example to see the folder that contains the selected file, Touch the curvy backward pointing arrow that appears in the upper-left corner of each file system window. You can see these arrows in the figure to the left.

Note: Do not keep an external USB drive connected unless you are using it. It continues to draw battery power even if the Nexus-7 is sleeping.

15 - Wrapping Up

We have barely scratched the surface of the Nexus-7 and the Google Universe. There are many other apps that you will want to know about, but this book is getting too big to include any more here. I believe that apps like Gmail, Persons (Contacts), Calendar and Clock work in a manner so much like other similar apps that you can probably figure out how they work just by experimenting.

In preparing this book I have found the Google and Nexus websites to be invaluable sources of up to date information. If you have a question, try doing a Google search on your question. You are sure to find dozens of pages of help - some of it actually useful.

As I mentioned at the beginning of this book, the Nexus-7 is one portal into the Google Cloud Computing Universe which is growing every day. There are other portals. In particular the line of Chromebook laptop computers is very popular. They are powerful and inexpensive. And they will seem very familiar if you are used to the Nexus-7. Shameless plug: I have written two other books on the Google Cloud Computing Universe covering Chromebooks and the Chrome web browser. If you are interested you can find these books available from Amazon. The titles are:

"Cloud Computing with Google Chrome", and
"Cloud Computing with Google Chrome - Volume 2"

I believe that you would find useful information in these books even if you do not own a Chromebook. A lot of what is in those two books deals with Google services that are available to you using your Nexus-7 just as they are available to people using Chromebooks or the Chrome web browser. I do cover Gmail, Contacts, and Calendar in those books. In addition, Google drive includes a set of apps that allow you to create word documents and spreadsheets and you can learn more about them in these books.

Thanks for buying and hopefully reading my book. If you found useful information in it I would appreciate it if you would take the time to go to the Amazon website and give the book a good review.

www.ingramcontent.com/pod-product-compliance
Lightning Source LLC
Chambersburg PA
CBHW080421060326
40689CB00019B/4332